Introduction	5
No Silver Bullet No Secret Sauce	7
This Agile Thing	11
Succeeding with Agile	12
Focus on Business Value	*13*
Viability	*18*
Incrementing	*22*
Iterating	*23*
Incorporating Customer Feedback	*24*
Organizational resistance to Agile	25
Reducing Risk	*26*
Thinking about adopting agile?	29
The Agile Team	30
Engineering Team	*30*
Scrum Master	*31*
Product Owner	*32*
Product Managers	*32*
Agile Coaches	*33*
Agile Ceremonies	34
Backlog Grooming	*34*
Shaping	*34*
Planning Sessions	*35*
Iteration Commitment Sessions	*35*
Daily Stand-Ups	*35*
Demonstrations	*36*
Retrospectives	*36*
CompStats	*38*
The Story Point	42
What are Story Points	*43*
Interchanging Story Points and Time	*44*
So, what's the problem?	*44*
Are story points good for anything?	*45*
What about T-Shirts	*46*
Feedback Stories	*47*
Bad things to do with Story Points	*47*
Metrics in Software Projects	49
Selecting the right metrics	50
Outcome Metrics	*51*

  Diagnostic Metrics *53*
  Confusing Diagnostic and Outcome Metrics *55*
  Activity vs. Effectiveness *57*
  The place for diagnostic metrics *58*
  Metrics Can't Tell you everything *59*
  Getting it wrong in the real world *60*
Using Metrics 61
  Metrics for comparing teams *62*
  Metrics at the Individual Contributor level *64*
  Metrics at the Engineering Leader Level *66*

Engineering Productivity 67
Defining Productivity 67
Measuring Outputs 68
Measuring Quality 72
  What qualifies as a defect? *73*
  Not all defects get reported *74*
  Not all defects are equal *75*
  Defects aren't immediately reported *75*
  Contained Defects *76*
Reframing the productivity discussion 76

Waste 80
  Waste Collection First Steps *81*
  Investments to improve quality are not waste *83*
Waste for teams to address 85
  Leaked Defects *86*
  Broken Builds *87*
  Refactoring *87*
  Production Support *89*
  Feedback is not waste *89*
  Planning is not Waste *89*
  Training is not waste *90*
Waste for organizations to address 90
  Hardware *91*
  Tools not bought but being paid for anyway *91*
  Tools you build when you could buy *92*
  Build and deployment *92*
  Virus Checkers *93*
  Environment issues *93*
  Communication Bandwidth *94*
  Excessive Planning *94*

Defense of Diagnostic Metrics	*94*
Analyzing non-actionable Metrics	*95*
Decision Making	*95*
Unnecessary Meetings or attendance at meetings	*95*
Constant Interruptions	*96*
Personnel Changes	*96*

Environment for Improvement 99
The Organization Paradigm Shift 99
   The Pain *100*
   The Vision *100*
   The First Steps *103*
Establish E2E Ownership 104
Staffing and Organizing 105
   Engineering Leadership *106*
   Engineering *108*
   Cross Functional Groups *111*
   Architecture *112*
   Project Management *112*
   Testing *114*
The Waste Management Process 120
   Identify waste buckets *120*
   Allocate buckets to teams and organization *120*
   Define Standard Waste Values *121*
   Create Collection Mechanisms *121*
   Begin Collecting Waste data *121*
   Establish Improvement Targets *122*
   Prioritize Improvement Initiatives *122*
   Reporting Waste *122*

Reducing Waste 127
Managing Quality 128
Definition of Done 130
   Make Technical Debt Transparent *134*
   Restrict Technical Debt Growth *138*
   Getting your Definition of Done right *139*
   Updating your Definition of Done *140*
Managing Defects 140
   Defect SLA *141*
   Contained Defects? *143*
   Intentionally Leaked Defects *144*
   Learning from Defects *144*

Resolved Defects..*145*
Continuous Integration and Deployment..146

Conclusion..147

Introduction

I tell my teams "Smart people learn from their mistakes and brilliant people learn from other people's mistakes – so, if you want to be brilliant you can listen to me and learn from my mistakes". I know that experience is usually the best teacher but sometimes it isn't necessary to make every mistake yourself to learn. Certainly not everything in this book is a direct result of a mistake, or at least of a mistake that I might have personally made, but what I do share are the learnings and experiences of my decades of experience in the software development business. My goal is to share things I have learned so that you, the reader can leverage, or at least consider my learnings as you face situations similar to those I have faced throughout my career. One particular area of focus is on our ability to predict software projects and concurrently on our ability to be able to actually measure how well we are doing and whether we are improving.

Throughout the book, wherever possible I use the word **leader** rather than **manager** and draw distinctions between **Engineering Leaders** and **Project Managers**. I also intentionally use the word **defect** rather than **bug** when referring to errors in software. I also consistently use the term **code complete** to mean code that the engineer believes is ready to be deployed to the live site rather than just meaning coding complete and now testing can begin. I draw your attention to these distinctions because when it comes to execution I believe they are critical differentiators in how we approach our trade. Understanding these differences and staffing projects with the right type of people is among the most important things you can do to ensure your projects will be successful. It is easy to hire managers, it is much more difficult to hire leaders. Managers are appointed to their positions, leaders emerge and are looked up to. It is easy to hire and train great project managers, it is much more difficult to hire and train great engineering leaders. You can go to university to learn everything you need to become a great project manager but it takes years of experience working as a software engineer to become a great engineering leader. With regard to the defect rather than bug distinction I believe we are long past the point where we treat engineering defects as cute little things like the moth that Grace Hopper discovered in 1946 in the circuitry of the Mark II.

I am neither anti manager nor anti project manager certainly both are needed and it is hard to imagine projects being successful without both. As I explain in a later chapter, project managers have a role on projects but it is in managing projects and not managing engineers or as members of agile development teams. Software development is something that needs to be managed monitored and tracked, however, there has to be a realization that software development is not the same as building a house. **The belief that more management or more people will lead to meeting more deadlines with higher quality is just not true.** There are things we can and must do to ply our craft more effectively but more people, more project managers and more management are not the answers. What we need to be doing is empowering and equipping our teams with the tools and education they need to be successful removing the obstacles that are in their way and measuring the right things.

I attempt throughout this book to present experience-based learnings and avoid the dogma of any single methodology. I present my perspective on what I've seen be successful and always try to do so from the perspective of someone who has been in almost any role you can imagine across the industry.

The book is organized in sections. The first section discusses agile and what it means to an organization. I give my perspective on how successful agile teams and projects execute and what the business can realistically expect to see from a high performing agile organization. The next section discusses the use of the metrics we need to effectively execute and continuously improve our execution of software projects, taking into account the realities of the software development world and the businesses we exist to support. I also assert that a majority of the metrics most projects use are meaningless in most contexts and propose how you can best assess and improve your team's execution. The final section takes a non-dogmatic look at some of the things we can do to make our teams more effective which leads to improving our ability to be as productive as possible.

Comments and questions are always welcome at john.belbute@gmail.com

No Silver Bullet No Secret Sauce

> When I moved into my new home one of the first things I did was buy myself a new push mower. Everyone else in our neighborhood had gardeners and truth be told so did we. But unlike my neighbors, I chose to mow my own lawn and to do it with a push mower. True, the lawn isn't that large but it would still take about an hour to do the job. One day my gardener asked me why I wanted to mow my own lawn when he could take care of it. I don't think he really understood when I explained to him that to me, mowing the lawn was a therapeutic exercise. I told to him that mowing the lawn gave me great pleasure because unlike my day-job, when I was mowing the lawn I could see exactly what I had accomplished and could see exactly how much I still had to do.

For as long as we have been developing software we have struggled to predict how long the development of a system is going to take and how much it is going to cost. We struggle with quality and even struggle to define exactly what it is that we need to deliver. Hardly a single project exists that has not suffered from some disappointment relating to cost, schedule quality or scope. The larger the project the bigger the problem. The problems can be any combination of quality, cost schedule or scope creep and often increase exponentially as the size of the project grows. The one thing we almost always do know is that there is a business need or at least some business value in having the system operational as soon as possible, an expectation that there will be no defects and a budget and schedule we are expected to stay within. This is the reality everyone involved in software development business has faced since the industry's inception.

While we've solved numerous problems in the software industry, predictability of scope, schedule, quality and cost linger. At the same time, the systems we are being asked to build are becoming more complex and the expectations of our users have increased and are rapidly evolving. Gone are the days where large investments in hosted solutions locked companies into a product for years or decades. We simply must get better and more efficient at developing and evolving the products needed to run our businesses. And more than ever before, the business of developing software has become the enabler for the business itself. The demand for engineers who can develop the software we need and for the engineering leaders needed to successfully lead implementations is greater than ever before. This all translates to companies being more and more dependent on software that they either license or build themselves. What is certain though is that whether you are a producer of software a consumer of software or both, the cost of software represents a significant business expense.

While consumers of software can focus on items such as features, price, performance and reliability of what they choose to license; producers of software are faced with the challenge of developing compelling solutions that they can license to their consumers. Escalating development costs combined with the ever-present pressure to develop software more predictably and efficiently understandably creates an environment where people throughout the business are constantly shining a light on their software engineering teams. It is completely understandable for the business to demand commitments and want to understand and control costs but we have never been able to capture that one metric that can tell us whether we are getting better at what we do.

It is this shining light that has and continues to drive the evolution of software development and software development management methodologies. Yet for all of the best efforts of many of the industry's smartest minds, we have still not found a way to become anywhere near as predictable and reliable as other areas of an organization. While those of us involved in the business of developing software understand that there may never be a perfect solution, those less directly involved in the actual sausage making want and sometimes demand to know. As development teams we are almost always forced to provide estimates of how long "it" is going to take and how much "it" is going to cost. Because we are forced to give an answer we always caveat our estimates with 'this is an estimate not a commitment'. In spite of whatever caveats we may assert though, the estimates somehow seem to be chiseled into stone, of course without the accompanying caveats. Inevitably, this leads to stress and conflict which then leads folks to look for new approaches to scoping, estimating and execution techniques that do provide the certainty the business demands but so far none have. Success of new approaches on pilot projects leads folks to believe the holy grail has finally been discovered only to find that what worked for one team on one project does not work for another team on another project, or even for that same team on another project.

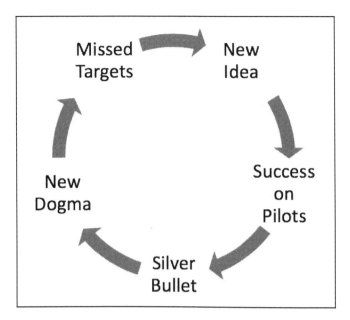

Figure 1 - For as long as we have been developing software we have been in search of the perfect methodology but it remains elusive. Nevertheless, there seems always to be the next development that people believe has cracked the nut

This has not stopped the search for that silver bullet or that cookbook answer that will ensure every project that following the recipe will deliver on time on cost on scope and with quality. Indeed, there are **No Silver Bullets**, and there is **No Secret Sauce**.

We jokingly ask "quality, functionality, time; choose two" but it isn't really a joke, the continuation of a project or even the continued existence of a company can be put at risk when large projects fail. There are certainly projects that deliver high quality on time on budget and with the agreed on functionality but they are few and far between. The road is littered with both estimation and execution methodologies and technologies that held the promise of solving the predictability problems. To date none of them have succeeded. Yes, there have been claims made that some of the approaches are successful but these claims can generally be attributed to either the creators of the technologies who are trying to sell you something, or to people who have adopted the technology and want to tout the positive impact of their decisions. This is not to say that there are not things we can do to improve our delivery capability, there are and I will discuss some of those. But the important point that this book is going to make is that while there are things we can do to improve our delivery, there is neither a silver bullet nor a secret sauce that we can sprinkle on a project to make it entirely predictable. What we do is hard and complex and the best thing we can do is accept this as fact and make the best of the situation. As I will repeat many times, **experience is inevitable but learning is not**. Billions of dollars have been wasted on consulting, technologies and tools that held the promise of solving the world's software engineering predictability and delivery problems but none have been the answer. Rather than continuing the quixotic quest for that silver bullet we are better served by expending our energies applying the learnings from our experience to manage expectations and improve our execution. We can't let the pursuit of perfection become the enemy of progress.

No doubt, as a software development industry we are in a better place today than we have ever been. Agile methodologies and technological developments have gotten us to the point where Continuous Integration has become a reality for many teams and Continuous Delivery is a reality for some and an objective for others. Unfortunately, though, the advances we have made have not lessened the business' desire to move faster with more predictability and reduced costs. Companies would be negligent if they did not pursue continuous improvement and that means you have to measure. But we have to both do and measure the right things and it is in those areas where we as an industry continue to under-perform.

While we might not yet want to acknowledge defeat in the search for the perfect methodology, one that ensures a 100% accurate solution to predictability on software projects, our energies are better expended by leveraging the things we have learned to do the best job we can. What we need to do is leverage the agile paradigm, be smart about the way we plan and execute set the correct targets for our teams and leaders, start measuring the things that it makes sense to measure and do everything we can as leaders to make our teams as productive as they want to and can be. We need to focus our efforts on the things we can improve and stop wasting time on items that don't move us forward.

This Agile Thing

The Agile Manifesto was published in 2001. It lays out a set of values and is accompanied by 12 guiding principles for executing in an agile fashion. In and of itself it is not a methodology but many methodologies have emerged embracing the values and implementing the guiding principles to various degrees. The most popular of all of these methodologies are probably Scrum and Kanban.

> ## The Agile Manifesto
>
> We are uncovering better ways of developing software by doing it and helping others do it. Through this work we have come to value:
>
> **Individuals and interactions** over processes and tools
> **Working software** over comprehensive documentation
> **Customer collaboration** over contract negotiation
> **Responding to change** over following a plan
>
> That is, while there is value in the items on the right, we value the items on the left more.
>
> © 2001, the Agile Manifesto authors
> This declaration may be freely copied in any form, but only in its entirety through this notice.

Figure 2- The values presented in the Agile Manifesto represented a transformative change from the traditional waterfall methods of developing software

In most cases, teams that adopted agile methods and practices improved their ability to deliver after a period of time. That said, predictability of project cost and schedule and the question of project scope still present challenges. Many organizations still struggle to develop the software they need as rapidly as they need it and organizations that have traditionally been in a waterfall development life cycle often still struggle with the reality that agile brings them no closer to being able to answer the questions of "When am I going to get what I want and how much is it going to cost?".

Fundamentally agile enables organizations to deliver software in a manner that reduces risk by rapidly and incrementally delivering the software that provides the greatest amount of value to the business. Organizations that succeed with agile focus on delivering quality working software as soon and as often as possible. They achieve their success because they:

- Understand what constitutes a viable product
- Focus on the highest business value items
- Increment
- Iterate
- Incorporate consumer feedback

Software projects do not succeed or fail because of the particular methodology they choose to follow. That is as true today when discussing agile methodologies as it was 20+ years ago when discussing the voluminous prescriptive waterfall methodologies[1] such as Ernst & Young's Navigator™ or Accenture's Method/1™. For that reason, I will not discuss Scrum, Kanban or any other methodology directly. All of the methodologies have their advantages and the dogmatic adherence to any of them does not guarantee the success of a project. **We score no points and deliver zero business value by rigidly following any methodology.** We only succeed if we are delivering value to the business. This means we are putting quality product in the hands of our consumers. That is not to imply that methodologies are bad, they certainly are not. However, the rigid adherence to methodological dogma of any sort is no guarantee of success and may even distract from the outcomes that are the most important.

Succeeding with Agile

Organizations that succeed with agile or any other methodology do not succeed because they rigorously follow a methodology. They succeed because they focus on a set of guiding principles and not dogmatically on a methodology. They succeed because they understand what constitutes a viable product, they focus on constantly delivering what is of the highest value to the business,

---

[1] My assessment of the methodologies and certainly not one that the proponents of said methodologies would agree with

they listen to their consumers and incorporate their feedback, they iterate and they increment. They succeed because they create environments where their engineering teams can be as productive as possible. They are laser focused on what is important, measure and monitor the right things and empower their teams by giving them equal doses of authority and responsibility. They also succeed because they create operating models that drive responsibility into the teams.

The principles behind the agile manifesto speak to the early and regular delivery of working software. There are many ways to deliver incrementally, but within an agile environment we associate early and regular delivery of software as initially delivering a usable product (viable) that has less than the full set of functionality and then adding (incrementing) to that functionality over time on a regular basis (iteratively). We might describe this as not delivering all the bells and whistles on day one and then adding the bells and whistles consumers ask for (incorporating user feedback) until what is being asked for provides less business value than delivering a different feature or product. Successful companies have product leaders who understand when they reach the point where adding more features is not the same as delivering a better product.

Focus on Business Value

Whether we are developing software or just going through our personal to-do lists it always makes sense to work on those items that are most important first. In an agile world that means we always have our teams working on the highest business value items in their work queues. There are a number of work item queues almost always available for agile teams. Figure 3 illustrates some of the more common queues. The most obvious queues are those containing stories supporting features but there are additional queues for feedback items and several classes of defects and potentially for experiments. During each sprint planning event teams need to review the items at the top of each queue and select the items they are going to include in their upcoming sprint. Product Owners need to maintain prioritized queues of all classes of work items as illustrated in Figure 3. For feature queues it is important to ensure that sufficient backlogs are maintained. If we are to always be working on the highest business value items then we need to be sure that the highest business value items are both defined, and in a state where teams can begin working on those items. When insufficient backlogs are maintained teams are either forced to work on less valuable areas of the product or in the worst case end up being totally blocked.

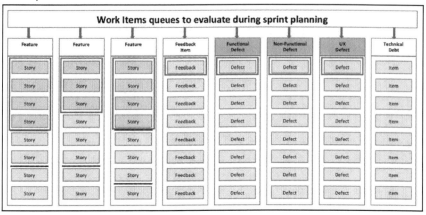

Figure 3 - All teams need to maintain work queues for a variety of items and as part of their sprint planning process look at the top of each queue to determine which items they are going to commit to working on for that sprint

It is not necessary to maintain separate queues for each class of defect but it can be helpful to the team to do so because it serves as a reminder that we need to keep focused not only on the functional areas of the system but also on the feedback, non-functional and usability and technical debt aspects of their systems. The team may also want to periodically review the distribution of the queues from which they are taking work items from, not for the purpose of forcing a particular distribution but just as a reminder that there are indeed many sources to choose from when looking for the highest business value items. Note that in Figure 3 the comparisons are not necessarily at the granularity of individual stories, but between releasable units of functionality. We need to compare at this level because we always want to be making new functionality available to our consumers and we can only do that when we have releasable components and single stories are usually more granular than releasable components. It is also important when committing to work on a releasable component that the team fully estimate the effort involved in delivering the entire releasable component. It is also important that the team have everything it needs to be able to complete the releasable component. If the team is dependent on a resource or decision not available at the time the releasable component is being committed to then it is better to not begin working on the component until the resource is available or decision has been made.

It is true that in a perfect world we would like to be able to make every story available to users as soon as it has been completed but for a number of reasons that we will discuss the reality is very different. We do not want to be defining stories that are extremely large or that require an entire team to work on them because they become difficult to coordinate and track. There is also a morale boost to the team when stories are completed and they see that reflected on their burn-down charts. We want to be able to define our stories in granular ways that reduce complexity both from the perspective of the story and from the perspective of the team that needs to accomplish the work. What we need to do is to strike a balance between making every story one that provides business value to the user and can be released when complete but which is overly complex and stories that are so granular that we lose the context of what is being developed. That balance is to identify the sets of stories that, when completed comprise what I call a Releaseable Component[2]. This concept is illustrated below.

---

[2] As discussed later in the chapter on Definition of Done there are a lot of implications to how release components need to be approached in the context of Definition of Done

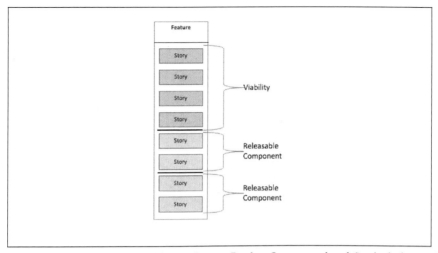

Figure 4 - Before beginning work on a feature, Product Owners need to define both the set of stories that constitute viability for a feature and then subsequently the sets of stories that can be released as groups

It is important that teams not fall into the trap of believing that they have to complete all of the releasable components in a feature before they move to the next feature. Teams need to commit to doing work at the releasable component level. This does not mean that the team has to commit all of the stories in a releasable component to a single sprint. Product Owners have a serious responsibility to define the stories in each feature that are needed for the feature to be viable and to also define the collections of stories beyond the point of viability that have to be released together. They do not have to describe all of the possible stories or even releasable components in a feature as long as what they have defined is viable. One practice that is sometimes followed is to define the known releasable components as a sort of "super story" and then consider breaking it into individual stories when or if that releasable component percolates to the top of the business value chain. Whatever we do though, we always want to avoid getting into the situation where a team turns a feature into a cottage industry.

Whenever a releasable component threshold is crossed within a feature the team needs to consider whether the next set of stories within that feature deliver higher business value than the stories at the top of the next feature's queue This concept is shown in Figure 5. When crossing releasable component thresholds, it is also important to consider whether feedback on recently completed features is likely to influence any new functionality being committed to and potentially delay any new work that might need to be changed as a result.

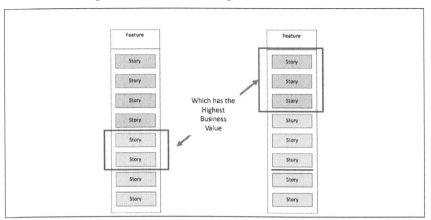

Figure 5 - Once a feature is viable product owners need to compare the next set of stories in that feature to the next feature's set of stories leading to viability to determine which alternative delivers that highest business value

The inclusion of items from low priority defects or feedback work items into a sprint needs to be based purely on business value. If resolving a low priority defect or addressing a feedback item has more business value than work on features then it should be addressed, if not it should be skipped over and reviewed during the next sprint planning session. An important consideration in the determination of which, if any defects provide higher business value than other items in queues has to be whether defect priorities have changed. This can happen vor several reasons but is common in cases where defects have a particular event horizon that is approaching. As discussed later, high priority defects are not part of the sprint planning process because they need to be addressed when they are reported. At the time a sprint is planned, the existence of high priority defects may impact the amount of work a team can commit to a sprint but addressing them needs to be non-negotiable and is defined in the operating model.

Viability

Viability at either the macro or micro level is achieved when there is sufficient functionality for the item to be usable and saleable. The definition of viability at the macro level is an organizational Product Management decision but if defined correctly it is the smallest number of features that can be released that deliver value to the consumer and that will allow the organization to start gathering feedback about what the consumer values. At the micro level feature viability is something Product Owners typically determine. In either case though, anything deemed viable and made available for users must meet the criteria specified by the organization's Definition of Done. Viable products provide the basis for the collection of consumer feedback.

There are many temptations for Product Managers and Product Owners to define viability as much more than it really needs to be. Often though it that they are fearful of making a bad impression with consumers who they believe will see the artifact as inadequate. While this is a legitimate concern, user feedback, in this case perhaps the fact that nobody was using the feature is sufficient to inform the Product Owner of the need to enrich the feature. More often than not, however, Product Owners tend to define more than is actually needed to achieve viability in a product including features that were either well beyond what was really needed for viability or, in the most extreme cases were even needed at all. There are many factors that go into defining viability at both the macro and micro levels but one factor needs to be how much and how often the releasable component is going to be used. It is often true that the most basic elements of a feature are the ones that are used by most of the users. Once viability has been achieved as additional releasable components are developed they are often used by fewer customers and sometimes are more difficult to develop.

Disrupt – because if you don't someone else will

As incredible as it sounds, I once sat in a meeting where a principle actually said "70% of our customers use only 30% of our product. We have to do a better job teaching that 70% what they are missing" to which someone commented "I think it's more like 80% only use 20%". Obviously if only 20 or 30 percent of your product is used by the vast majority of your customers then there is a likelihood that you have spent a lot of money developing software that is used by only a small percent of your user base. That may not necessarily be bad but in most cases, it is.

First, it's bad because if only 20% or 30% of your software is being used then another company who wants to disrupt would only have to develop 20% or 30% of what you have developed to compete with the majority of your customer base. So, with a relatively small investment competitors can capture the majority of your user base leaving you potentially with a much smaller set of users who stay with you because they need or use the most difficult to develop portions your software which are normally the most expensive features to develop.

Disruption takes many forms however, and particularly for companies that have established products, there is a strong likelihood that the disruption will be to internal processes and potentially even to other internal organizations. For example, many organizations have built extensive training and consultancy groups around their products. Arguably, these training and consulting groups are only needed because the product is too difficult to use or implement. I saw a poster once which said "a user experience is like a joke, if you have to explain it it's not very good". I would make a case that these training and consulting groups exist precisely because user experiences whether they are related to installation of the product or use the product are in fact outgrowths of our products not being very easy-to-use. So, it follows that if we do a better job developing systems that are intuitive and easy-to-use that the amount of training consultancy and of course documentation that will be needed we'll be a lot less then perhaps it exists in the organization today. This is certainly difficult for an organization which may be collecting significant portions of its revenue through these training and consultancy activities. It isn't always easy for an organization to adapt to a significant loss of revenue in such areas. Often these organizations that you will be disrupting have significant clout and we'll resist efforts to reduce or dismantle them.

Whether we are building an entirely new product, a replacement for an existing product or new feature into your product it is vital to get that product in front of users sooner rather than later. It is often the case that a product manager develops a particular affinity for a new piece of the product and defines that product's viability well beyond the scope of what would normally be considered viable. In the worst-case this can lead to significant amounts of engineering effort being invested into a feature that may ultimately flop.

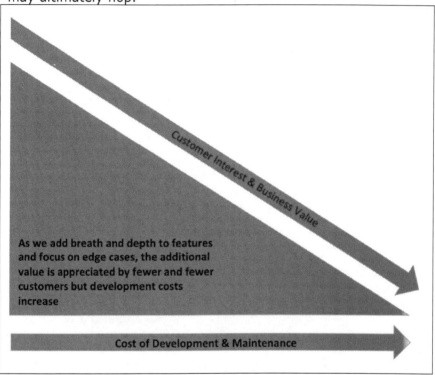

Figure 6 - Every line of code we develop costs money to develop and maintain. At the same time the additional functionality tends to be used by fewer users.

We've all probably seen the graphic that describes how to build agile. It starts with a skateboard and it progresses to her scooter and it progresses to a motorcycle and ultimately at some point in the future becomes an automobile. When looking at that diagram it occurred to me that if I were to apply that diagram to a problem I had once it would've led to an interesting consequence let me explain what exactly I'm talking about. I worked on a campus that was pretty sprawling and I happened to work at one end of the campus and my boss was at the complete opposite end of the campus. It was about 500 meters between the two buildings. It was not a rare occasion where I would have a meeting at my side of the campus that ended at the top of an hour and headed need to be at a meeting with my boss at the other end of the campus at the top of that our that my meeting at just ended. Going back to my diagram if I were incrementally building my transportation to get across campus the first delivery of the skateboard would have been an interesting Mode of transportation for getting across the campus. If I happen to be a really good skateboarder it might even have worked however on the path between my building and my boss' is building I had to cross several streets and go across several curbs all things through which skateboards are not particularly good. They're certainly not good if you are a beginning skateboard. So, the next iteration would've delivered a better capability which was the scooter and scooters are little bit easier to use than skateboards they require less balance they also lack the ability to effectively manage curbs but the solution that is at least viable for a majority of the population. The third iteration is the bicycle I Just about everybody in the world knows how to ride a bicycle. Bicycles are inexpensive, they navigate curves reasonably well. Bicycles are faster than skateboards are scooters and they are easy to park. So, this is where I think the entire situation gets very interesting because we're incrementally delivering and it may be that long before we deliver the product we originally envisioned as the end state we have actually achieved the optimal state. Anything more than a bicycle starts to not only be overkill but also starts to introduce problems as people need special licenses for motorcycles and parking for automobiles present challenges. So, by following an iterative approach to incremental delivery we actually arrive at the optimum solution long before the envisioned and state.

Embrace Disruption

The importance of correctly defining what constitutes a viable product can make or break a project. I am aware of at least one instance where the insistence by a Product Manager and the agreement by the CEO that a particular feature be complete before a product could be released set the release date back by nearly six months ultimately dooming the company. Viability has to be addressed on two levels, what I call the macro level, the smallest number of features needed for a product to be viable and what I call the micro level, the minimum amount of functionality needed for a particular feature to be viable. When all of the macro level features have reached the point where they are viable the product is ready to be released to consumers. Delaying release beyond that point in time only delays the opportunity to begin learning and collecting feedback and also leaves the door open for competitors. Some will argue, particularly when a product being developed is going to compete with an existing product, that releasing a product with fewer features or less functionality is doomed to fail but this argument has serious flaws. The biggest flaw in the argument is the fact that if there are already competing products users will not be interested in the less featured competitor. Folks making that argument though are missing the point and fundamentally don't understand disruption. No potential customer is forced to start using a product with fewer features but if they do choose to do so then it may be an indication that the existing products have features that are not all that important and that an opportunity to disrupt the existing products exists.

Incrementing

Defining and delivering viable features and products is important because it allows us to get product in front of customers quickly. It also rapidly gives us the opportunity to begin learning and potentially also allows us to disrupt. Rarely though will the viable product or feature be the final state of the feature or product. In an agile environment we expect to add to our features over time and also to add new features to our products. Sometimes as soon as a viable feature or product is released the sequence of what comes next is already defined, other times what comes next will be dictated by consumer feedback and still other times by changes in the business environment.

When to stop incrementing?

Teams need to have ownership of one or more project components. Ownership over time results in improved business acumen by all members of the team and helps the team develop pride in their work products. It also leads to any defects that are discovered being resolved more expeditiously than they could be by any other team but also in a manner that is more likely to result in a higher quality engineering solution.

The danger relating to associating teams with one or more product components is that teams can sometimes turn their components into cottage industries where the team is just continually allowed to keep developing new functionality for their components. Across the board in agile environments we want to always have our teams working on the highest business value items. We want to ensure we are doing this whether it means having a team move from one feature to another, resolving a P3 defect rather than taking on a new story or moving to an entirely new area of the product rather than continuing to develop an area that already has more functionality than is possibly needed. It is the responsibility of Product Owners, Product Managers and Engineering leadership to ensure that cottage industries are not created. To do this they need to regularly ask themselves whether they are committing to a feature or story because that feature or story is of high business value or because there is excess bandwidth on the team.

To avoid turning teams into cottage industries organizations need to create a mechanism that periodically takes a high level look at the Releasable components that are being worked on to convince themselves that none of the teams are working on items that are of little business value and if necessary redirect the team to work on other areas or products.

Iterating

In a scrum environment, iterations are synonymous with sprints. Even in environments that are primarily Kanban focused we tend to see iterations. Iterations effectively create time boxes that push teams in the direction of delivering workable software at the end of each iteration. Most teams that adopt scrum choose a duration between 2 and 4 weeks for their iterations. For teams using Kanban there are no specific iterations although it is quite common to see a hybrid model emerge where the flow of work through the sprint is managed using Kanban techniques.

The more teams move in the direction of Continuous Delivery the more the concept of iterating becomes blurred because software can end up getting delivered when it is complete.

Incorporating Customer Feedback

Listening to customers is something all successful companies do. Feedback is very constructive because it helps us improve our products. Over time it has become increasingly easier for customers who are unhappy with one vendor's product to simply switch to another. Systems have become more and more open and the ability to export from one system and import to another system has become easier and is almost ubiquitous. This easy ability for customers to switch between vendors has made listening to customers increasingly more important. Today almost every product provides users the ability to provide feedback.

But not all feedback comes directly from user-initiated messaging. A large portion of feedback gathered in today's environment is gathered by collecting user behavior data.

Users want to be heard and listened to. If you are going to institute a feedback loop it is a good idea to let your users know that you are listening to them.

It is important to differentiate between feedback and defects. User feedback is a good thing but hearing from users that the product is broken, while important to hear about, needs to be dealt with differently than constructive feedback.

Scenario	Feedback or Defect
Call center is receiving calls complaining that the search function is slow. Telemetry shows that users are abandoning the site but all SLAs are being met.	Feedback – The team had done what was needed to develop and validate that the software met the SLA. The SLA was not aggressive enough to satisfy user expectations.
Monitoring indicates that a new deployment of a service has raised CPU utilization requiring additional instances of the service to be deployed	Defect – The fact that a new release has necessitated additional servers indicates that there is a performance defect that the team failed to contain.

Scenario	Feedback or Defect
Log data indicates transactions are failing due to a data validation error.	Defect – Software should reject a transaction that has invalid data rather than just trying to insert the data into the database.
When releasing a new version of a product an outage impacting all users is necessary even though the Definition of Done requires updates without user impact.	Defect – Violations of non-functional requirements are no different than functionality that does not work.
Behavior data indicates that users are taking more than one minute to complete a task that has only 4 steps	Defect – if the requirement specified an SLA that is being violated Feedback – if no SLA existed and the issue was detected by analyzing user behavior data

Figure 7 - It is important to differentiate between defects and feedback because work on defects is rework which takes away from productivity and work on feedback is productive

Feedback is not Scope Creep, it's being agile

Earlier in the book I discussed the fact that in addition to being unable to predict cost or schedule that we also have difficulty in addressing scope. In an agile world scope, and scope creep in particular are interesting concepts that deserve discussion. There are clearly many ways to look at scope creep but I find it useful to categorize expanding scope by the source of the scope with the two sources being product and users.

Organizational resistance to Agile

Companies like predictability, they do not deal well with uncertainty. It follows then that when it comes to software development they want to know when a product is going to be done, exactly how much it is going to cost to develop, exactly what it is going to do and how much they can sell it for. There is nothing inherently wrong with any of these desires and it might even be considered irresponsible not to care. However, given the number of variables involved in software projects, predictability is something difficult to achieve. Agile does not attempt to provide any of this certainty. In fact it does just the opposite. This leads many companies, particularly those developing their own internal systems, to struggle with the move to agile. In many cases the issue comes down to what is perceived to be a lack of commitment on the part of the development organization. In other instances it comes down to the question of "when will we be done?". When a company needs to make a major investment in either an internal development or one that it sells to customers, the agile versus waterfall discussion almost always ensues.

Imagine you are the person having to write a check to finance a major initiative. Two proposals are in front of you. The first proposal is from the waterfall camp. In the proposal there is a promise that a specific set of features will be delivered on a specific date for a specific amount of money and with the promise of high quality. The second proposal, the one from the agile camp promises that at any given point in time they will have delivered working software and be working on the highest remaining business value elements of the project. There is no promise that everything will be delivered by a certain date but there is a commitment that at any point in time what will have been delivered will be working and will deliver business value.

To the person writing the check there is a lot more commitment coming from the waterfall camp than there is from the agile camp. What the person signing the check is hearing from the waterfall camp is "We promise to deliver this on this date for this price" whereas from the agile camp they are hearing "You get what you get when you get it". This apparent inferior commitment from the engineering team sometimes makes the person signing the check reluctant to support the agile proposal.

Reducing Risk

Of course, it is true that agile does effectively promise that **you get what you get when you get it**. But if you look at the waterfall model it also gives you what you get when you get it. The difference between the agile "you get what you get when you get it" and the waterfall "you get what you get when you get it" is that agile promises to deliver working software more rapidly than waterfall does, and, if the engineering teams are executing smartly what does get delivered are the highest business value items. Certainly people who understand and have delivered agile projects understand all of this but the difficulty we continue to have is project progress and status reporting that can compete with what waterfall methods provide. The milestones that come with waterfall are absent in an agile environment and it is sometimes difficult for organizations to grasp the concept that none of what were the traditional development milestones exist, even though the milestones were mostly meaningless with respect to how projects were progressing.

Perhaps the biggest advantage of agile though is that if reduces the risk that teams deliver large amounts of software that are not what the consumers want. One way to think about this is to imagine getting on an airliner to fly across The United States from Boston to San Diego. It is about 2,583 miles and is expected to take about 5 hours and 23 minutes flying at a heading of 271 degrees. Now imagine your pilot takes off sets the course at 271 degrees and for the flies for 5 hours and 23 minutes lowers the gear and lands. How likely would it be that he would hit the runway? How close to the San Diego airport do you think they will be? Clearly no pilot would ever do that. They would look regularly at their instruments and adjust course and re-vector themselves regularly to correct course to ensure they were always heading in the right direction.

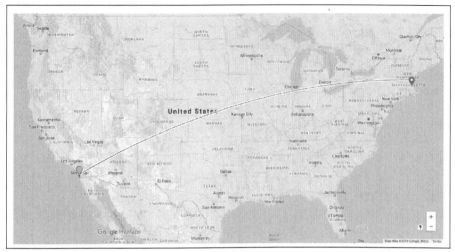

Figure 8 - Not too many people would want to be on the plane flying from Boston to San Diego that had a pilot flying at a heading of 270 flying 5 hours and 23 minutes lowering the gear and landing and hoping that we were at the San Diego airport but that is effectively what waterfall methodologies offered

It is probably worth noting that while agile is a relatively new concept in our software engineering community that the ideas of incremental and iterative delivery combined with incorporated user feedback have been around for at least the last three or four decades. What has changed is that frameworks such as Scrum and Kanban have emerged which have formalized some of the activities and made the concepts more popular.

While we might all agree that incremental and iterative delivery of software and the incorporation of user feedback are the right things to be doing and that by embracing the agile manifesto and adopting the associated principles we can get software into the hands of our consumers more rapidly we have to agree that agile can not ever provide the certainty of scope and schedule that companies desire. As engineering leaders, we need to have the courage to resist the temptation to promise what we know can not be achieved.

We still see projects that are late, over budget, suffer from poor quality and that don't meet user expectations. The solution can't be in more rigid processes or more adherence to methodologies. We've tried that with things like CMMI, TSP/PSP and a variety of other approaches. The answer has to be somewhere else. We have to realize that pure Scrum or Kanban and explaining to the business that you are going to get what you get when you get it, even though that is ultimately always going to be true irrespective of the method followed,

There are no points for perfectly executing on any methodology. We only win when we can improve our execution. At the same time, we need to find ways to give our project sponsors the confidence that we are indeed constantly improving our execution and that confidence has to be demonstrable and quantifiable.

Thinking about adopting agile?

The decision to adopt agile is a big one. Those of us that have been doing it for years and have seen the advantages of agile are convinced. But most of us have also seen the difficulties of doing so. Adopting agile involves a major paradigm shift on the part of the organization when it comes to scheduling and predictability. Project Managers often struggle with the shift as they see agile as "you get what you get when you get it". Indeed, some engineers even believe that to be the truth. Engineering teams that have been working in a waterfall model generally embrace agile as they see it as an opportunity to reduce the amount of documentation they need to produce. Some teams even see the move to agile as the opportunity to be freed of deadlines. Often they see it as an opportunity to be more self-directed and organizing and in some ways as engineering being put in charge of the direction of the product.

Adopting agile is not always easy. It is a difficult change management problem and all change is hard. Like all big organizational change it needs to be carefully planned. Communication about the change, what the impacts on each part of the organization are and what the future state will look like are all necessary ingredients of a successful adoption.

The Agile Team

The heart of any agile organization are the teams that develop products. Normally a team is responsible for an area of the product. As the agile manifesto states, Individuals and Interactions are highly valued so creating teams comprised of highly capable engineers who interact well together is critical to the team being successful. Teams are most successful when they are self-organizing and self-policing. They set high bars for themselves and place the success of the team ahead of anything else. They develop business acumen in their areas of responsibility and have pride in their work. When a member of the team is not performing up to the standards the team has set for themselves they are not afraid to confront a non-performing member of the team and in some cases even vote a team member off the island. Teams generally perform best when their membership remains static over the long term.

Ideally, teams are units that in the course of a sprint are not dependent on any resources that are not full time members of the team. External dependencies on specialized skills such as User Interface or User Experience designers need to be resolved prior to a team committing to any stories and while the external resources may be consulted with during the course of the sprint any such consultation should never be of a nature that it could cause the team to have to stop working on a story.

Engineering Team

Engineering teams are typically comprised no more than seven engineers with nine being the top end. Engineering teams should be kept together for as long as practical. While there will almost always be a mix of skills and experience on the team it should always be the case that anyone on the team is generally capable of working on any story in the team's backlog. Everyone on the team and who attends the daily stand-ups and other ceremonies needs to be a pig[3]. There are no chickens on engineering teams.

---

[3] The pig and chicken metaphor refers to an old fable of unknown origin used to describe the difference between commitment and involvement. The Pigs who are totally committed and the chickens who are only involved. Another way to think

There will almost certainly be folks on the team with different skills who for the most part need to be capable of filling in for each other. The notable exceptions to the rule are the role of the Product Owner who in most cases is not an engineer and of the designated tech lead. Whether the Product Owner is a part of the team within the organization's reporting structure is not important as long as both the team and the product owner understand that one cannot succeed without the other and that they will either fail or succeed together. The tech lead role is generally assigned to the most capable engineer on the team. In some cases the tech lead has a dual role as they may also have the responsibility of engineering management for the team. It is also common to have the tech hold the dual role of architect. Whether the dual roles are a good idea or not is debatable and depends a lot on the personalities of the individuals on the team and indeed on the personality of the individual themselves. The Scrum master is another specialized role on the team. The Scrum master role is best filled by an engineer on the team who has received additional training in the responsibilities of the role.

Scrum Master

The Scrum Master is the person on the team who helps the team by leading the execution all of the scrum ceremonies and who ensures that any blockers encountered by the team are quickly resolved. The Scrum Master role is not that of the team lead or engineering leader and the team does not report to the Scrum Master. Scrum Masters are most effective when they are full time members of a single team. Some organizations choose to mix the position of Engineering Leader and Scrum Master however this can infringe upon the openness and interactions of members on the team during scrum ceremonies.

Product Owner

Product owners are the primary representatives of the business and must have the ability to make decisions during sprints about it is in the context of breakfast where the pig has to sacrifice himself to provide the bacon but the chicken just has to lay the egg.

without having to go to anyone else. A Product Owner who does not have the authority and responsibility to make decisions is merely a conduit to a decision maker which results in teams waiting on decisions but which also leads to the product losing the respect of the team as they are seen as not empowered. Product owners need to be empowered by Product Managers and be delegated equal amounts of responsibility and authority to if they are to be successful. Product owners are responsible for prioritizing and managing team backlogs, triaging defects and leading the sessions where story points are assigned.

The most successful Product Owners are the ones that are able to always prioritize the highest business value items in their work queues, listen to their users and know when to say "enough is enough" when either deciding what constitutes viability or deciding when additional functionality is no longer adding significant value to the product.

Product Managers

Product Managers are not part of scrum teams but the role of the Product Manager is critical to the success of any product. Product Managers have numerous responsibilities in the organization but from the perspective of the engineering organization the most important thing Product Managers do is to provide a vision for the Product Owner and teams to follow. There are many techniques to expressing a vision, however, most of them are very sterile and boring and thus lack an inspirational component. The approach I find to be the most effective is written as a newspaper article that looks back on the system when it's an operation once is actually been developed and is being used by its users. This approach is particularly motivational as the members of the engineering team have the ability to understand where the features and stories they are working on fit into the bigger picture. It is absolutely critical for a Product Manager to empower the Product Owners that interface with the engineering teams.

Agile Coaches

Some organizations choose to engage agile coaches to help either with their transition to agile or to improve their teams' execution. Agile coaches are not actual members of scrum teams and are often externally contracted resources. Some companies make a business out of providing agile coaches.

When selecting an agile coach it is important to be clear about what you expect to achieve through the engagement and that you are confident that the coach you select is going to be able to meet your expectations. Keep in mind the fact that there is no proven recipe for project success. There are certainly practices that will increase your team's probability of success but there are no guarantees. If the coach or organization tells you what your problem is or what the solution to your problem is before you tell them what you are trying to achieve then you probably have the wrong person or organization.

When considering engaging an agile coach it is a good idea to use a sports metaphor when thinking about the relationship between a coach and an athlete or in this case between the coach and the team. Coaches and athletes develop a love hate relationship. The coach spends a lot of time observing the athlete and tells the athlete what they need to change to get better. The coach's feedback to the athlete is constructive criticism and nobody likes criticism even when it is constructive. The athlete knows that the coach is there to make them better but at the same time the athlete is giving it his or her all and still not being good enough for the coach. In the end when the athlete's performance improves they are appreciative of all the work the coach did even if the path to improvement had been difficult. The power of direct observation and the openness to provide the team with the honest feedback they need to improve are the key elements we need from our coaches. Our teams though have to be open to listening to and acting on the sometimes difficult feedback they get from their coach.

Agile Ceremonies

Scrum identifies five formal ceremonies, Backlog Grooming, Planning Sessions, The Daily Scrum, Demonstrations and Retrospectives. While these are the formal Scrum ceremonies the additional activities of Shaping and CompStats are also important for improving the efficiency of the team's execution, the former to ensure that the flow of work to the team is kept constant and the latter to provide the team with a mechanism for reviewing their diagnostic metrics.

Backlog Grooming

Backlog grooming is an activity that is driven by the Product Owner. It is quite common to for the Engineering leader to participate and other members of the team may also be selectively included in the sessions but it is rare for all of the members of the team to participate. The purpose of Backlog Grooming is to ensure that stories are kept up to date and that changing priorities are adjusted prior to planning sessions with the entire team.

Shaping

Shaping sessions are not formal Scrum sessions but they do formalize the process of ensuring that Releasable Components are defined to the point that there is a reasonable expectation that all dependencies outside of the team have been resolved before the entire team gets involved in the planning process. Shaping sessions are the responsibility of the engineering lead and may involve other members of the team as well as representatives of other functional organizations that are not dedicated members of the engineering teams. DevOps is one example of an external team often included in the Shaping sessions and is particularly critical when any new technology is being introduced into the environment.

Planning Sessions

Planning sessions are used by engineering teams to estimate the complexity of items in their backlog. Only members of the engineering team including the product owner should be in attendance. The Product Owner takes the lead in presenting the stores and the items from the various work queues to the team which then discusses the work needed to implement the story and estimates the relative complexity of the story as compared to a set of reference stories that the team has already completed. This process is generally referred to as story pointing. The team also wants to ensure that any story they address is one that they could immediately begin work on should they choose. In other words, before a story can be pointed any preparation or dependencies on other teams have been resolved.

Iteration Commitment Sessions

At the beginning of every iteration the team meets with the product owner to commit to what they are going to accomplish during the iteration. The team should only commit to items that are ready to be completed without any outside help. The team is responsible for ensuring that all defect and support SLA requirements are committed to and worked on in accordance with the SLA before any new work is committed to. At the end of the meeting the team will usually publicize what they are intending to accomplish during the iteration. During the iteration commitment session it is the responsibility of the Product Owner to ensure that the work the team is committing to is of the highest business value. Figure 3 shows a list of work queues that need to be considered when determining which items are going to be included in the iteration.

Daily Stand-Ups

Daily stand-ups are generally meant to last 15 minutes or less and are mandatory for all team members. The stand-ups provide the members of the team with the opportunity to share their accomplishments, plans and obstacles with the entire team. The

Scrum master is the person who leads the meeting and all members of the team are expected to be present at each of the meetings. During the daily stand-ups the Scrum Master asks each of the team members three questions:

1. What have you completed since our last meeting?
2. What are you planning to complete before our next meeting?
3. What are your blockers?

Demonstrations

In many ways the highlight of every iteration is the demonstration which occurs at the end of the iteration. This is the team's opportunity to showcase what they have accomplished in front of a larger audience than just the team and the product owner. Product Management and other members of the larger team can be invited to the ceremony and should be invited to provide feedback. There should be no surprises during the demonstration from the perspective of the team or the product owner. It can be helpful for the team to also point out stories that were added to the backlog as a result of feedback. The team may choose to mention the fact that in addition to having completed the stories that were committed to that they also resolved several defects, however the resolution of defects, while necessary should not be celebrated. Demonstrations can also be used to give the engineers on the team the opportunity to highlight the work they personally did during the iteration.

While demonstrations are generally an end of iteration event there can also be significant value in using demonstrations in the course of an iteration. This is particularly useful when a team is working toward a challenging delivery goal and the user interface is highly interactive. By increasing the cadence of demonstrations and opening them to larger product audiences teams can benefit by the increased amount of feedback.

Retrospectives

Retrospectives are a formal ceremony for Scrum and may well be used in non-scrum environments as well. The purpose of retrospectives is to look back over a period of time, usually a sprint, to discuss what went well and what went not so well during the period and to agree as a team what you are going to change. Retrospectives tend to be more subjective than objective and generally are not an analysis of any metrics the time might have generated. It is often said that experience is inevitable but learning is not. Retrospectives provide teams with a structured opportunity to turn their experience into actions so they can learn and improve. Any team that was interrupted during the increment to provide either production support for an incident or that was compelled to interrupt their iteration to address P1 or P2 defects will also want to discuss what they might have done to have prevented any such defect from having leaked. For retrospectives to be successful they need to be attended only by the members of the team. Sharing the results of the retrospective with others outside of the team is something that should certainly be done as it both makes the team feel more accountable to make whatever changes they decided were necessary but it also provides the opportunity for other teams to perhaps learn from the mistakes of others.

Retrospectives also provide a vehicle for teams to highlight organization improvements, particularly any that are slowing the team down and thus generating waste. Engineering leaders need to ensure that any such incidents are placed in the Organizational Waste Reduction backlog.

I led a project that had 12 scrum teams for about 40 sprint cycles. Teams were all expected to conduct and document the results of their retrospectives on the project wiki. Participation in retrospectives was restricted to members of the team and all of the team members were expected to participate. In reviewing the results of the retrospectives there were several patterns that clearly emerged:

1. Teams were identifying the same problems over and over again.
2. Teams were committing to long lists of improvements they wanted to make.
3. Teams were often looking to point out problems that were outside of their direct ability to control.

To a large degree, what had happened is that the teams had let their retrospectives lose value. They were sometimes being held just because they were 'supposed to do them'. It actually became obvious that we were not actually getting any benefit from the retrospectives. To refocus the teams and get back to the point where retrospectives were beneficial we introduced a process change and asked the teams to identify only one change they were going to make and then to make a discussion of their execution of that change the first agenda item in their next retrospective.

At the same time, assuming they are valid, the issues the teams raise that are outside of their control need to be addressed by the organization. This is particularly true when the items are things that are contributing to increasing waste. A real example of such an item occurs in many organizations where top technical talent is pulled out of the team to work on tiger-teams or special projects. While it may be necessary and in the best interest of the organization to take such actions, as will be discussed later, such actions are disruptive to the team.

CompStats

Unlike retrospectives, CompStats are not formal agile ceremonies. CompStat stands for Computer Statistics. It is a technique that was originally developed by the New York City transit police and was implemented at the city-wide level by police Commissioner William Bratton. What Bratton did was to use real data to display interactive graphics to study crime and policing statistics to identify areas where changes in policing behaviors could either help police reduce crime or respond more effectively to it. What Bratton was doing was interactively looking at different dimensions of a situation together with his team and brainstorming how they could improve their performance.

In our engineering environment, CompStats are the vehicle we use to look at what we did to accomplish our objectives.

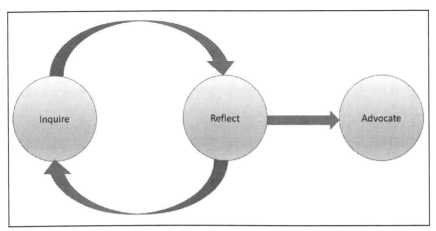

Figure 9 CompStats are a coaching activity so achieving the desired outcome means we have to resist the engineer's bias to solving a problem and lead the team through the process of coming to their own conclusions

In an agile world, or for that matter in any software development environment, we use CompStats as a coaching activity to look back at the execution of a team focusing first on its outcome metrics and then reviewing what the team did or did not do in the process of achieving their results, and how effectively they did or did not do things to achieve its outcome. This is where the diagnostic metrics collected throughout the development cycle come into play. It is important to use the CompStat process as a learning activity and also to have at least one person participate in the CompStat who is not part of the team. In an agile environment at the very minimum the Scrum Master and Engineering Leader need to participate. There is certainly no harm in having additional members of the team participate or indeed to have the entire team participate. CompStat sessions are not something engineering leaders use to punish teams with and if done properly should be something teams look forward to. For CompStats to become and remain effective they cannot turn into inquisitions. As with any coaching activity the participants from outside the team need to go through the cycle of inquiring and reflecting, leading the team to arrive at its own solution before advocating for a change. As engineers this can be difficult as we are by nature problem solvers and tend to just jump immediately to advocating for a solution. While we do not want to use CompStats to ridicule or otherwise punish the team for what they did or did not do, we do want to keep in mind that being a coach means sometimes having a love-hate relationship with the team. The team might hate to have a light shined on their mistakes but will appreciate the improvements in their performance as a result of the coaching they receive.

Every environment is different but, in any environment, there are tools and techniques engineers and teams use to develop their products. Things such as Code Review tools, automated testing tools, defect tracking tools static analysis tools, code profiling tools and code coverage tools are some of the most common tools used across the industry.

Throughout any sprint or release cycle, teams will use some or all of the tools available to them to various degrees and with various degrees of effectiveness. To get the most out of the tools it is important to select tools or devise methods to capture metrics about the tool usage and results. The data gathered during the period of time you are reviewing is what you will use during the CompStat review.

Keeping the focus on outcome metrics is important but there are things we can do, levers we can pull if you will, that may influence your outcomes. So, if the team did well we might look at what practices the team employed to achieve its outcome and conversely if a team did poorly what they did or did not do to achieve their outcome. Let's look for a moment at a specific example.

Imagine you have a team and during an iteration that team was able to achieve its committed story points. Throughout the iteration there were no leaked defects that the team needed to address. This obviously is an ideal situation and certainly a situation that we would like all our teams to be in. Using the CompStat methodology, we would interactively review the actions the team took throughout their sprint to achieve the outstanding results. We might look for example at how many code reviews were conducted, perhaps by whom and how many defects were identified and remediated as part of the code reviews, again perhaps by whom. We might also look at how many code improvement suggestions were made and implemented as well. We might also look at the unit tests that the team had written, perhaps the amount of code coverage the unit tests achieved and review whether those unit tests had found any significant code defects. We might also want to look at whether there was correlation between the complexity of methods and classes and the use of unit tests. We might also look at whether the team had cleaned up any Sonar Cube violations that were identified by the automated inspections and maybe look for patterns and trends that could be identified. It is important, particularly when looking at anything related to asynchronous defect activity, or the absence thereof, that they look back over several iterations as the time between when a defect is introduced and when it is discovered can be considerable. The possible items you can look at are only restricted by the capabilities of the tools that the engineering teams use throughout the SDLC.

In conducting CompStat reviews you always want to keep the objectives in mind. CompStat reviews need to be treated as learning experiences not as opportunities to punish or embarrass a team. You want to ensure that you do not get into a situation where the team dreads the next CompStat. Ideally, the team might want to eventually begin conducting their own CompStat reviews. What is critical though is that when conducting CompStats you avoid the trap of turning a diagnostic metric into an outcome metric. To declare, for example because a team achieving excellent productivity had been formally reviewing 90% of their code that all teams were required to review 90% of their code would be a mistake. I have often explained this to teams by simply explaining that if I were to tell a team that they had to do a particular number of code reviews during a sprint, or develop a specific number of unit tests during a sprint, or peer review all of their code during a sprint and they did all the things they were told to do but at the same time they failed to achieve their outcome objective then they would be justified to assert that they had done exactly what they had been told. They would of course be correct. More important though would be the reality that by proscribing these kinds of actions what you actually create are two issues, one for the team and one for yourself.

From the team's perspective you will have disempowered them. They will no longer feel empowered to do what they think is correct to achieve the outcomes they are targeting. They will be pushed into a corner where they are doing things because they were told to do them, not because they believe them to be the right thing to do.

From your perspective, if you start to dictate how much of everything a team needs to do then the problem that you had given the team no longer belongs to the team but rather it belongs to you. A key rule that all leaders should have is that they should never delegate responsibility **OR** authority, they should always delegate responsibility **AND** authority.

The Story Point

In an agile world it is sad but almost impossible to have a conversation about metrics without having Story Points enter into the discussion. It is important though that when having any conversation that references story points that there be a clear understanding of what they are and are not.

When we see the number 10 we automatically assume it means the number of digits most people have on their two hands. That is because almost everything non-geeks do is by default assumed to be in the decimal system. In reality though, what that number or any other number represents can be broken into components. Starting with the low order digit (the one just to the left of a decimal point) what any number really represents is the digit * the numbering system raised to the zero power which will always equal one. Proceeding to the left then the next digit is the number of units of the numbering system raised to the power of 1 which will always equal the numbering system, then the digit * the numbering system raised to the power of 2, etc. So, our traditional 10 is really $0*10^0 + 1*10^1$ (the number of digits on two hands). Similarly, if we were working in binary where there are only two digits available what we normally think of as 10_2 would be $0*2^0 + 1*2^1$, or 2_{10}, (the number of thumbs we have on our two hands) and in octal where there are eight digits 10_8 would be $0*8^0 + 1*8^1$ or 8_{10} (the number of fingers we have on our two hands). I could go on but suffice it to say, that in Hexadecimal 10_{16} is equivalent to what we generally think of as 16_{10}.

What, you ask do numbering systems have to do with story points? Well, imagine you have a project with 3 teams, one responsible for the registration area of your product, another team responsible for the billing area and another team responsible for accounting. Each team estimates their stories for their upcoming iteration and coincidentally all have both an 8 point and a 13 point story in their sprints. We might look at the pointed stories and think that there was an equivalent amount of complexity but that would be incorrect. What we really will have is that the registration team will have stories of $8_\text{registration}$[4] and $13_\text{registration}$, 8_billing and 13_billing, and $8_\text{accounting}$ and $13_\text{accounting}$. Because each team's estimates are using a different numbering system it is impossible to perform any mathematical operations on the numbers.

What are Story Points

Story points are values assigned by a team to a story that represent how complex the team estimates that story to be. Story points are arbitrary measures that are assigned based on a team's relative ranking of the complexity of the story they are assessing as compared to other reference stories they have completed and to which they have assigned baseline values. Generally, teams assign points to a story based on a modified Fibonacci scheme so values of 0.5, 1, 2, 3, 5, 8, 13, 20, 40, 100. Because we want the reference stories to have meaning to the teams, each team selects their own reference stories. They then compare a story that they are about to work on to stories they have already completed and assign the value they agree on. All members of the team are expected to coalesce around a single number. Often the voting is done using planning poker cards where each member of the team is given a card with each of the values in the sequence and then when asked by the Product Owner each member shows their card. Because it is important that the team provide the best estimates possible we need the teams to provide their own reference stories. It is highly unlikely that any two teams would use the same reference stories although in cases where a team is being split in two to seed other teams this could be the case. So, because all teams have different experiences and will use different reference stories as baseline values and have different levels of experience, no two teams are likely to assign the same number of story points to a given story, and that's ok. Indeed, if a team were to point a story today and then for whatever decided to revisit the point estimate in 6 months it is entirely possible that they will assign a different value to the same story. This could be as a result of a

---

[4] We generally assume all values expressed as digits are in base 10. When any other numbering system is used, by convention we express that base as a subscript. I have used that convention here to illustrate the concept that the raw digits in the example are each in their own numbering system.

number of factors including additional experience or maybe turnover on the team but it really does not matter. Fundamentally story points have one and only one value and that is to provide the team a mechanism for determining how much work they are going to commit to during an iteration.

Interchanging Story Points and Time

Unfortunately, when teams size stories they express the complexity as a number. Numbers almost always find their way into spreadsheets, which almost always leads to having those numbers used in formulas and ultimately to measure time. It is a trap many projects fall into and there are even tools on the market that will do this for you. The problem though is that interchanging story points and time implies a level of specificity that is greater than the mathematics support. The mere fact that teams generally use the modified Fibonacci scale when estimating complexity should be enough to convince anyone that applying a formula to such a broad estimate is incorrect. It is certainly possible that given enough data about completed stories that a mean could be calculated that would allow time estimates to be calculated based on stories that had been pointed, however to do so would require teams to record the time they spend on stories which is something that as explained elsewhere is not easy to do.

Interchanging story points and time can also lead to a lot of spreadsheets being generated and to people external to the team believing they can swap things in and out without consequence. It would be ridiculous to get into a situation where someone outside of the team dictated replacing one 13 point story with 13 one point stories. Mathematically that works but story points just don't work that way.

So, what's the problem?

Imagine now that we have developed a backlog of pointed stories for each team and we were to compare the story points of one team to the story points of another team. For simplicity's sake let's just assume that each team has a backlog of 100 story points. What I have not told you though is what numbering system each team used to arrive at their respective 100. So if we were to assume that one team used octal, one used decimal and one used hex then while each team had declared 100 story points, for the team using octal the 100_8 was equal to 64_{10}, the team using decimal the 100_{10} was equal to 100_{10} and the team using the hex 100_{16} was equal to 256_{10}. When the numbers make it into a spreadsheet everything is calculated in decimal. It is confusing enough when we do this with numbering systems where we have the science of mathematics behind us and the base of the numbering system can be known and understood, in story pointing nobody outside of the team understands the base and unlike numbering systems it is subjective at best.

Are story points good for anything?

Story points are used by the team to estimate and commit to what they are planning to accomplish in an iteration. Outside of the team, or when looking cross team there is little real value in story points. There are no mathematical operations that can be computed on story points. It is not possible to exchange thirteen one point stories with a single thirteen point story. As long as story points are understood to be a currency that only has value on a single team's island they have value. However, it is important that everyone understand that they are not absolutes. With respect to acceleration over time using story points it may be interesting as long as the scope of any analysis is at a single team, however there are numerous other factors that also need to be considered and as will be discussed later, high priority defects leaked in prior iterations can significantly impact the story point values as a metric of either accomplishment or acceleration.

Where story points may provide value outside of the team is in the area of monitoring backlogs. Earlier while discussing Agile Ceremonies and in particular Iteration Commitment Sessions I stated that the team should only commit to stories that are ready to work on and for which no external dependencies need to be resolved. In order for the teams to be able to do this they need to go into those commitment sessions with backlogs that are at least as large as their average sprint velocities. It makes sense for the organization to track the size of the backlogs of their teams so that they can take any actions they can to avoid teams entering commitment sessions without an adequate backlog. Story points and moving averages of teams velocities should be used to calculate the number of sprints worth of backlog each team is maintaining. The number that is important is the number is sprints worth of pointed backlog items and not the actual number of story points.

What about T-Shirts

T-Shirt sizing is a technique that is sometimes used very early in the development of a product or feature to provide a ballpark estimate of just how much effort is going to be needed to develop the product or feature being scoped. The result of T-Shirt sizing efforts is to assign a T-Shirt size (S,M,L,XL,XXL) to the anticipated effort. The sizes are meant to be very rough estimates usually expressed in a combination of person and calendar months of how much effort and time might be needed to deliver the feature in question. T-Shirt sizing can be very helpful when Product Management is making strategic decisions about whether or not to proceed with development of the functionality. When working with T-Shirt sizes it is important to be transparent about the degree of confidence there is in an estimate. If, for example a Large T-Shirt is the equivalent of a seven person engineering team working on a feature for up to six months then that estimate should also have a confidence factor associated with it, say +/- 25%. The larger the T-Shirt size the larger the confidence factor should be.

T-Shirt estimates do not need the involvement of the entire engineering team. In most cases product management and engineering leadership can collaborate to come up with the appropriate estimates.

It is perfectly reasonable to associate the T-Shirt size assigned with a ballpark size amount of effort. The key component of that statement is that it is very much a ballpark estimate. The danger with T-Shirt sizing arises when an organization tries to treat the T-Shirt size as something more specific than it can possibly be. This is something that can be seen among organizations that decide to associate T-Shirt sizes with story points. Doing so is a clear indication that an organization is using story points in an inappropriate way. When this happens there is always going to be a tendency to turn the story points into a budget for the teams that will eventually have to do the work. When this happens there are a number of potential consequences and almost all of them are bad.

Feedback Stories

Feedback stories should be pointed as any other story however it does make sense to at least be aware of the fact that a story is a feedback story as well as whether the source of the feedback was product or user feedback. The decision of whether feedback stories should be pointed is an interesting one and one. From the perspective of the team and the planning of an iteration the answer is clearly that feedback stories need to be pointed. On high performing teams the commitment to the content of a sprint is motivational and we do not want to do anything that will detract from the motivation. At the same time, as I will discuss later, there can sometimes be a fine line between feedback that is of a positive nature and feedback that is of a negative nature.

Bad things to do with Story Points

There are lots of bad things you can do with story points and certainly any time you use story points in a scope larger than a single team there is something wrong. That said, there are some things that are absolutely wrong. Without a doubt, the most destructive thing you can do with respect to story points is allow for them to be used for remediating leaked defects. Any team that story points defects is creating the illusion that they are doing something productive when in fact what they are doing is completing something they already said was complete. In those cases where teams are allowed to story point defect remediation activities it is an indication that the teams and perhaps the organization are more focused on banking story points than they are on actually delivering business value and a quality product in the first place.

A Real-World Bad Example

A Director an off-shore operation has decided that his teams need to double their productivity. He measures productivity as the number of story points the team delivers. As I have pointed out at length, story points are arbitrary measures, and as also pointed out, if there are numbers they are likely to end up in spreadsheets and used to make conclusions that are often incorrect.

All of us would love to find ways to double the productivity of our teams. But what exactly does it mean to double the productivity of our teams. This particular Director believes that if teams can double the number of story points they are banking that they will be twice as productive. There are numerous strategies to achieve the doubling of the number of story points the team can bank but none of them correlate to improved productivity. One strategy might be to take advantage of the arbitrary nature of story points and ask the team to recalibrate their story points so that the same amount of work would be categorized as twice as many story points. This would double the number of story points being banked per sprint without in any way altering the amount the team was actually producing. Another strategy might be to ask the team to work twice as many hours. While both of the strategies seem ridiculous at best, the director has chosen one that is potentially even more ridiculous, destructive and misleading than those. He has determined that's the best way to double the teams' productivity is to have the team story point the fixing of defects that they leaked. It's certainly true that if a team is spending half of their time resolving defects that they have leaked that by allowing the team to point the defects that they are resolving that they will showing increased in the number of story points that they are banking each sprint. It goes without saying either of these approaches illustrate the danger of treating story points as absolutes. It also completely violates the idea that waste is a bad thing. Indeed, the illusion created by the apparent doubling of any team's productivity could lead to folks outside of the engineering community to conclude that the director is being highly effective, when in fact what he is doing is farcical. What the directors approach actually does just to say I don't care about waist all I care about is the number of story points banked.

Metrics in Software Projects

It is important that as engineering leaders we are always able to answer 3 simple questions:
1. Are we better now than we were?
2. Are we going to be better than we are now?
3. How will we know?

Irrespective of the methodology we follow we need metrics to do our jobs. If we aren't measuring something the only reason we have to believe we are getting better at what we do is foolish optimism. Nobody wants to be thought of as a foolish optimist. Metrics are key weapons in any performance measurement and continuous improvement tool kit but like any weapon they can be used properly or improperly. Too often in software environments the wrong metrics, for example story points, are selected or the right metrics are selected and then used improperly. This can be true in any environment but it is particularly true in software development environments where there is always pressure to deliver more predictably and faster and where processes generate lots of data and there is an abundance of resources capable of automating the collection and analysis of the data.

Whether you are getting started with metrics or already are using them on your project to be successful you must be transparent about why you are collecting the metrics you've chosen and what you intend to do with the metrics you collect. It is always best to be open and transparent about what you are doing as a leader and when using metrics one key to whether you will be successful or not is transparency. People often fear metrics and if too much focus is given to a single metric it is likely that the metric will drive the wrong behavior. Nothing could be worse than a team "hearing through the grapevine" that some metric is being collected and that it is being used for something other than what it actually is being used for. It is much better to be forthcoming, even if there is a potential that some folks may be unhappy with the choice or application of your metrics of choice. The best and most enduring way to achieve this transparency is to formally publish and adhere to a Metrics Policy where you specifically state what you are hoping to accomplish with your metrics program as well as the context you will collect and use your metrics.

Figure 10 contains a sample of such a metrics policy.

> Sample Metrics Policy
>
> On our project we are dedicated to a culture of transparency and continuous improvement. For that reason, we collect and analyze a number of metrics throughout our Product Life Cycle. The metrics we gather are used for process improvement at the organization level. We commit to being completely transparent about the metrics we collect and how we use them. We forbid all punitive use of any of the metrics we gather at the Individual Contributor level. The use of process improvement metrics by any member of the management team at the individual contributor level will result in disciplinary actions up to and including termination. The metrics we gather together with their application is kept current on the project wiki.

Figure 10 - A Metrics Policy that explains what you are doing and how you are going to work with what you gather can go a long way to improving the quality of the data you will be able to gather and in the way the team responds to the initiative.

Selecting the right metrics

Selecting the right metrics for your environment is not just about seeing where there is some activity that can be measured and then starting to collect and analyze the data. This is true across the board but particularly true in a software development environment. There are lots of things we can count and track but for a metric to be helpful rather than just a number we have to understand what we are going to do with it and what behaviors we are trying to drive with it. We also have to understand the nature of the metrics we are using and whether the metric is an outcome metric, something we are trying to achieve, or a diagnostic metric, a measure of effort rather than results. This is the most important distinction we need to make when we look at any metric and one that must be clear before beginning any serious discussion about what metrics you are going to collect and how you are going to use them. It is important to remember that if a metric gets published it is going to attract attention and discussion. If too much focus is given to a single metric it is probably going to cause teams to focus their efforts on improving that metric without considering the consequences of the impact on other metrics that may be equally important. Often times discussions can lead to lengthy debates that do absolutely nothing to advance either the state of a project or the performance of a team. When this happens we end up increasing the amount of non-productive time being spent on a project.

Indeed, we all need metrics to do our jobs and to improve our ability to execute. But to be successful in collecting and analyzing our metrics so that we can achieve the outcomes we are targeting we must use the right metrics in the right way and in a positive way. We also have to be sure that we are analyzing metrics in the appropriate context and scope.

In general, though it is always important to remember that the best way to destroy your ability to use metrics for improvement is to use your metrics for punishment. As leaders we are not rewarded for doling out punishments, we are rewarded for executing and improving. Not using metrics in a positive way, or focusing on a single metric without understanding the full context of what is being analyzed creates pressure and often leads to gaming the system. Another common failure is to focus on metrics that measure effort rather than outcomes. We do not want to collect and use metrics just for the sake of collecting and using metrics. We collect and use the metrics that are available to us because we want to diagnose and improve. Succeeding with metrics means using them for learning and improving. To be successful as an engineering leader you must be able to have confidence in the data you are using to make your decisions. That means you must have reliable telemetry that everyone believes in. Too often people spend more time debating the validity of the measure rather than using the data to make the improvements we all want and need to achieve. Bickering about whether a value was correctly recorded or whether it is something that has value does not move us forward.

Outcome Metrics

Let's first address what outcome metrics are. Our outcome metrics are the most important metrics we have. Outcome metrics are the ones that if we improve on we deliver more value to the business. We're talking about software development and largely in an agile world but let me stress that the outcome metrics in any context are those things that you want to achieve. In a business context an outcome metric is directly in support of a business goal. Increasing revenue or profitability are examples of business goals. The outcome metric does not have to be identical to the business goal but it must have line of sight to the business goal. Outcome metrics are not about the effort we invest or the activities we perform to achieve the objectives, they are purely about the results we achieve. Another way to think about outcome metrics is that they are the things your project sponsor cares about. This is a very important concept and one we do not want to forget. So, if we look at a typical agile software project, what are the outcome metrics we want to achieve? In most environments where things are being constructed the goal is to produce as much high quality product as quickly as possible. In most contexts this relates directly to velocity (how much are we producing and are we improving our capability to output more) and quality (how good are the things we are producing and are we improving the quality). Without yet getting too much into the use of velocity and quality in a software environment, it is easy to agree that we want to deliver a lot of business value and we want what we deliver to be of high quality. We also want to continuously improve the amount of what we produce and the quality of the products we produce. There may be other outcome metrics as well and there is a lot of granularity in the velocity and quality categories that can be defined as well but in a software development environment your outcome metric must address producing something of high quality and over time increasing the amount of output and improving the quality of those outputs and over time.

As I will discuss later, because both the quantity and quality of the outputs of the software development process are nearly impossible to measure we are challenged to identify a meaningful outcome metric. We want to keep our outcome metrics separate from the diagnostic metrics, which while important for learning are not things we want to achieve. What we do to achieve our outcomes is important, but, if we could magically achieve perfect quality without investing anything to achieve perfect quality I think we would all be overjoyed.

An outcome metric for software development is not as difficult to define as it is for organizations to accept. The only metric that meets all of the outcome metric criteria is the percent of productive time the team spends on productive activities during an iteration. The reasons why this is the case are explained in detail the next chapter but conceptually it is relatively straight forward to understand that if we measure how much time a team invests in building additional functionality and over time drive to increase the amount of time the team spends on building additional functionality that we are doing the right thing.

Diagnostic Metrics

Diagnostic metrics are measures of effort or resource utilization expended in support of achieving an outcome. It is useful to think about diagnostic measures as what we did with the levers we had available to us to influence the outcome. In a software engineering environment we have a number of levers available to us. The tools and processes we choose to equip our teams with and the tools and processes the teams choose to use are all chosen to help deliver increasing amounts of increasingly superior product. The degree to which those tools are used though, while worthy of analysis in some contexts are not, in and of themselves outcomes or anything we want to specifically set objectives for.

In other words, you will never be able to say that if I increase a certain activity, ex. Code Reviews or Unit Testing, by a certain percent that there will be a corresponding impact on the quality outcome. In so many words, diagnostic metrics have no linear correlation to how many points we put on the board. The degree of correlation between a diagnostic metric on one team is not likely to be the same degree of correlation when we look at another team, Diagnostic metrics may be interesting and useful in CompStats and at the team level but they are not something that your Project Sponsor probably cares about. Project Sponsors might care about how much time a team wasted fixing leaked defects but probably not about how many code reviews were conducted.

Coming back then to our agile software development environment to look at examples of what diagnostic metrics are and why they are also important let's look first at some of the diagnostic metrics supporting the quality of our outputs. I begin discussing the quality diagnostic metrics because they are very illustrative of the distinction between outcomes and diagnostics but also because they are easy to understand and are quite often falsely treated as outcome metrics when in fact they are not.

In the quality space there are numerous diagnostic metrics available to us. All of them relate to some activity the team performs that they believe will reduce the probability of them leaking a defect. Some of the more common ones are:

- Number of Unit Tests
- % of Unit Test coverage
- Number of formal code reviews conducted
- % of new or changed code formally reviewed
- Number of UI tests created
- Number of open Blocker and Critical inspection issues not addressed
- Performance and Characterization tests

and of course, there are many more. What they all have in common though is that by tracking any of them or by increasing the amount on any of them there is no direct correlation between the efforts expended and the outcomes achieved. It is also important to keep in mind that it is not about how much of any activity you do but rather how well your teams execute the activities. Indeed, if a team does more of any of the above correctly they are probably going to improve their quality outcome but the correlation is not at all direct. More execution is not the same as better execution.

In categorizing a metric as a diagnostic metric you are in no way asserting that the metric is not something we want to look at. Diagnostic metrics are not bad metrics but they are bad outcome metrics. They are extremely important metrics that tell us a lot about things including efficiency but in and of themselves they are not the outcomes we want to achieve. Many of them also look at counts rather than effectiveness, which is a discussion for later as well.

Most of the tools in our environment also collect their own metrics, some of which relate to the results of having used those tools. For example, if we look at Code Reviews, good code review tools collect data on the reviews. Depending on the tool you can see what was reviewed, who participated in the review, how much time was spent on reviews, how many defects were found during the reviews and other data that is valuable in analyzing whether the reviews were proving effective. All of the data collected by the tools can provide insight into the activity that went into using the tool but it is important that the data be looked at in the proper context.

Another way is looking at diagnostic metrics is by thinking about how we achieved our outcomes. Imagine that over a period of time one of your teams has an absolutely perfect quality outcome. They haven't had to interrupt their work to fix a leaked a defect in 5 sprints. None of the other teams have anywhere near that kind of an outcome. Wouldn't it be helpful to be able to look at the various practices used on the teams to leverage some of the learnings from the successful teams to help the lower achieving teams improve their respective outcomes? Conversely if there was a team that was achieving very poor quality and their diagnostic metrics showed no code reviews, no unit tests, no functional tests and no performance tests it would certainly be helpful to point those things out to the team. If you think about it, diagnostic metrics are the ones that tell us a lot about how we arrived at the outcomes we achieved. The diagnostic metrics play a crucial role during CompStat reviews and in coaching environments but their application needs to be understood. Observing that one team that has a near perfect quality record and which has 100% unit test coverage and as a result compelling all teams to achieve 100% unit test coverage is unlikely to result in other teams achieving the identical result.

Confusing Diagnostic and Outcome Metrics

Why is it so important that we be clear about what our outcome and our diagnostic metrics are? In case the answer is not obvious in fundamental terms, as leaders we need to focus on results not effort. We all want and need the engineers on our teams to give their best efforts all the time and while we appreciate effort the reality is that effort is not synonymous with success. Nobody wants to stand in front of their project sponsor and explain that we tried really hard we just failed. Everyone has probably had situations where there was a really nice engineer on their team that worked really hard but just couldn't deliver the outcomes we needed. If we measure effort rather than outcomes we run the risk of ending up with a team of really hard-working people who accomplish very little or nothing.

Irrespective of how we state the goals for engineering organizations and teams it is fundamentally about how much you are producing, how you are improving your ability to produce, how good your products are and whether they are getting better.

Imagine yourself a leader who wants to ensure their teams are delivering software of high quality. You might as many project managers or engineering leaders do prescribe to your team that they code review all of their code, that they write a certain number of unit tests for their code or achieve a specific percentage of code coverage in their unit testing or that they develop a certain number of automated tests for their code, or perhaps some other engineering practice be carried out to a specified degree. None of those goals for what are outcomes. They measure only effort. This is a perfect example of confusing diagnostic and outcome metrics. It is a bad idea. The thing that matters is how good is our quality and are we getting better? If we tell our teams that they must review all of their code, that they must achieve 100% percent unit test coverage with their automated tests or that they must carry out some other quality practice to a specified level then you lose the focus on the outcome you're trying to achieve.

That in no way means unit testing, code reviews or other engineering practices aren't things that we want to be doing and should be doing. Any of the practices probably help improve the quality of the products we construct. But if the team does in fact achieve the levels of those specific practices that we prescribed and we fail to achieve our outcomes who is to blame? The team would certainly be well within its right to push back and say we did what you told us to do and they would be right. What effectively happened was you as a leader disempowered the team by telling them how they had to execute not what they had to accomplish. You would have lost the focus on what was really important and instead replaced it with a prescription that in this example resulted in a less than optimal outcome. A better approach and one which recognizes the difference between what we want to accomplish and how we accomplish it is to maintain the focus on the outcome metric which in this case is improved quality and leave it up to the team to figure out how they are going to achieve that outcome.

Activity vs. Effectiveness

Addressing the efficiency of any activity is intuitively something we all want to do. But we must keep in mind the fact that in our environment efficiency of any single practice cannot be an outcome metric. It would be a mistake to create an efficiency target of an engineer coding a specific number of lines of code per hour or of a team finding a certain number of defects per hour invested in code reviews or for a team to achieve a certain number of story points over a period. An efficiency metric makes sense if we look at building widgets but not in a software development environment. It is easy for us to measure that in our factory today we have 10 widget makers who together produce 100 widgets per hour. If we could find a way to improve the efficiency of each worker so that they could produce one more widget per hour we could improve our productivity by 10% while increasing only the raw material costs. That is pretty easy to understand. It is hard to find a parallel instance of this type of efficiency in a software engineering environment.

In our software development environment we might look at our code review results and see that for every person hour we invest in code reviews on average we discover two code defects. So it follows then that if a team had leaked 10 defects in the previous sprint one could come to the conclusion that if they had spent 5 more hours on code reviews they would have not leaked any defects. This is obviously false. But the example illustrates some of the challenges we have when we look at the efficiency of any activity we perform that relates to a diagnostic rather than an outcome metric. In the case of the widget makers, the number of quality widgets produced per hour is an outcome metric where in the case of code reviews finding defects through code reviews is not the outcome we are looking for, rather, releasing code with fewer defects is. I'll also note that in this example that setting a goal of discovering 2 defects per hour during code reviews is probably going to drive the wrong behavior. How easy would it be for engineers to just inject a couple of extra easy to find defects so that the code reviews could meet their efficiency targets or to start reporting stylistic defects just to meet their targets.

Equally as flawed as setting efficiency targets for activities is the practice of setting count targets for an activity. It accomplishes nothing to set a target such as finding a number of defects through some activity. What would anyone actually do with such a target? Would teams keep looking for defects until they got frustrated and maybe just coded a couple so that they could move on? Or would they stop trying to contain defects when the target had been achieved? Both of these potential behaviors are wrong but if leaders confuse outcomes with diagnostics it is inviting such a consequence.

If we start to try to improve the efficiency of non-outcome activities then we effectively turn that activity into an outcome which is not something we want to do. As mentioned earlier, outcome metrics are those that directly support business outcomes. This is not to say that we should not have some of the efficiency data available to us, there is a place for it, but it has to be managed carefully and used in the right way. They should never become targets. There is a German word, 'Fingerspitzengefuehl' that does not exactly translate into English but which roughly means when you can decide on one of two outcomes because it is so hard to be exact having the ability to make the right decision at that point in time. When it comes to knowing when and how to use efficiency metrics for non-outcome specific results we all need to have 'fingerspitzengefuehl'. This subject will be discussed more when CompStats are introduced.

The place for diagnostic metrics

Many of the tools used by engineering teams do gather significant amounts of data about the use of the tools. Some of the data points correlate to what was accomplished by the tools. Examples of such items could be the number of issues found during code reviews or the amount of time spent in code reviews, the number and trends of various issues identified during SonarQube continuous inspections or the number of unit tests executed and the coverage achieved during the testing. Defect management tools can also often provide information about the types of defects that are being leaked. None of these metrics are outcome metrics but they may provide information that can lead to improvements that can lead to overall improvements. We would be negligent as engineering leaders to completely ignore this information. There are potentially opportunities to identify areas where training could either improve the team's use of the tools or reduce the number of issues being injected which, whether contained or not somehow impacted the amount of productive time the team was engaged in.

The best place to review the metrics from engineering tools is at the team level and every engineering leader should regularly do so. The second place where this and other diagnostic information can be reviewed is in the CompStat retrospectives.

Metrics Can't Tell you everything

It is not at all uncommon to come across a team or individual engineer that boasts that they are always achieving 100% unit test coverage on all the code they write. Sometimes this is because an engineer is particularly obsessive about doing so and that may be fine. In other cases, though, teams are compelled to do so as the team's Definition of Done makes 100% Unit Test coverage a requirement. In either circumstance the behavior is driven by the belief that by achieving 100% unit test coverage that quality will be improved and indeed perhaps it will. In any event, 100% Unit Test coverage is an often-misunderstood metric and a prime example of how achieving a diagnostic target fails to actually achieve the actual target.

More often than not 100% code coverage in testing is more of a Red Flag than it is a guarantor of high quality. First, 100% code coverage is extremely difficult to achieve. Achieving it generally means either there is an extensive use of mocking or that there is a dearth of error checking. Without a doubt, mocking is one of the best quality practices teams can employ to achieve high levels of quality. It is, however, expensive to universally implement correctly and in a Continuous Integration environment can add a lot of complexity to the infrastructure. 100% unit test coverage is much easier to achieve in those cases where there is no error checking at all in the code. Clearly, this is not a practice that any good engineer or team would follow, but, in the case of mandated 100% unit test coverage it is a behavior that can be encouraged and that has been observed.

The same can be said of other practices even including code reviews. Mandating that 100% of code be reviewed or inspected can be equally as wasteful. Indeed, code reviews are a great practice but is it likely that simple functions like getters and setters are going to contain errors? While reviewing code that is extremely simple is not necessarily a waste activity it is certainly effort expended that is unlikely to yield any positive result other than checking a box on a form.

The important thing to keep in mind is that teams need to be held accountable for their outcomes and empowered to achieve them as they see fit. They are closest to the work that needs to be done and therefore best positioned to decide how to achieve the outcomes we give them as targets. The Engineering leaders we put in place are ultimately accountable for creating the environment and culture that enables and drives the success of their teams.

Getting it wrong in the real world

I was an engineering leader in the central engineering organization at Intuit. The products that we built were either embedded in products built by other development groups or were services used by the company's products. Because our products were all used by multiple products the consequences and costs of failures was high. We decided to embark on a comprehensive quality improvement initiative. One of the things that we did was to train the entire team on the Fagan Defect-free process™, (Fagan Inspections). The Fagan inspection process is a rigorous process designed to contain defects and shorten the release cycle. The process is very well-suited to reviewing documents as well as it is to reviewing code. We took the decision to train the entire staff on how to do inspections and mandated that 100% of requirements documents and 50% of code be inspected. Several months into the initiative we were seeing inspections happen but were not seeing the improvements we desired. The buzz on the floor was that the teams were doing the inspections because they were told to not because of a belief that they were achieving the improvement goals. We were seeing neither the quality improvements nor the accelerations we were expecting.

This is a great example of using a diagnostic rather than an outcome metric to measure progress. It's also though a great example of selecting the wrong adoption metric. If we had heard the buzz on the floor to be that we were doing metrics because we didn't have the time to not do them we would have had a much more meaningful result than by compelling the teams to hit particular targets.

Using Metrics

Another important consideration when setting up a metrics program is understanding the scope of a metric's applicability. Generally, the rule of thumb is that outcome metrics can be applied at any level and rolled up to higher levels but that diagnostic metrics only add value if they are looked at in the context in which they are collected, usually this is at the team level. Because any of the diagnostic metrics are expressed as some kind of a number there is always going to be a tendency to put them into a spreadsheet either for summary or comparative analysis. It is easy to do this and while some summary information can be interesting that is only the case when the units being summed are identical across all the areas where they are gathered. For example, at the project level it might be interesting to know how many defects were contained through various engineering practices. That is of course because a contained defect is a contained defect regardless of which team found it. Other abstract concepts make no sense to either summarize or analyze. Story Points or lines of code are perfect examples of values that mean nothing when you add them up or compare them across teams.

The most common and harmful use of metrics is when they are used primarily with negative consequences or to beat people up. Using metrics when measuring at the individual contributor level is equally harmful. Improper use can take many forms, however, including measuring the wrong things, measuring too much or too little or focusing on a single metric that leads to driving the wrong behavior or using a metric in the wrong context. Imagine how easy it would be for a developer who was going to be measured and rewarded only by how many defects he or she leaked. Why would anybody in that situation risk missing a target by doing something foolish like actually writing some code? Indeed, this is an extreme consequence but it does clearly illustrate the single metric issue.

As we look at metrics in software related context, or probably any context, we want to remember the 3 questions we always need to be asking:
1. Are we better now than we were?
2. Are we going to be better than we are now?
3. How will we know?

Without metrics we are really flying blind though so we have to strike a careful balance. As engineering leaders, we need to use metrics even if ours are not nearly as exact as those available to the pilot of a modern airliner.

For any metric initiative to succeed, and by succeed I specifically mean lead to the desired improvement, it must drive the right behaviors without creating a lot of disruption or anxiety on the team. The metrics also have to be targeted so that they can be acted on at the right level. It does no good to measure an engineer on the company's profitability. That may be a good measure for a CEO but there is little if anything that a single engineer can do to impact that metric.

Metrics for comparing teams

Projects consisting of multiple teams often feel the need to have comparative objective metrics they can use to evaluate and maybe even stack rank their teams. It is not unreasonable to want do so but it is important to keep in mind that no two teams are assembled with equivalently talented or experienced individuals, no two teams face equally challenging problems at the same time and in many cases teams are not identically sized. As will be explained in detail later, in a software development environment the concepts of output and quality measurement at the source can not reasonably be measured. With those considerations in mind though it is worth looking at whether anything can be reasonably compared between teams both in terms of the quantity and the quality of their outputs.

Quantity of Output Metrics

We need to be extremely careful in how we use any metric and understand that a metric that may be perfectly ok to use in one context may have devastating consequences in another context. In spite of the fact that story points are arbitrary, many organizations look at the story point as a velocity measure. When taken in the context of a single team it may be interesting, albeit not actionable, to look at a team's story point velocity over time to understand whether there is some trend that can be observed. There are of course numerous factors that feed into the team's velocity but nevertheless there can sometimes be reasons for trends that are at least worth investigating. It is absolutely meaningless to look at and compare velocity between teams as measured by story points. As I discussed previously, story points are arbitrary and subjective and the idea that you could have an objective metric based on something entirely subjective is obviously flawed. I like to describe story points as a currency that is only useful on the island that is the team. There is no exchange rate for story points between teams. You might as well use coconuts on one island as the currency and pineapples on another or binary on one island, octal on another and hex on yet another. There is no official exchange rate between coconuts and pineapples. So, this is a perfect example of a metric that has value in one context, looking at a team sprint over sprint, but not in another context, comparing one sprint team to another. Using comparative velocity between teams will lead to lots of discussion and probably some arguments and likely some incorrect conclusions but it will lead to little else.

That does not mean it is impossible to compare teams and in the next chapter I will go into depth on the topic of waste as an actionable metric that can easily be used. However, for organizations that are not yet measuring waste, it may be interesting to create a simple inter team metric to track whether a team is meeting, exceeding, or missing the goals they set for themselves and by how much. When properly presented, as the percent of committed story points achieved during a sprint this may provide a normalized metric as it ignores the amplitude created by the arbitrary nature of the story point process. That said, while there may be something we can learn about the team dynamic and perhaps leadership by looking at the data it is important that we recognize that none of this data are outcome metrics and so from a comparison perspective they are simply not actionable.

Stressing that this metrics can never be treated as an outcome metric it may be interesting to track because it may provide some anecdotal information about whether the team is at least challenging themselves to improve. If for example you see a team that commits to the same number of story points every sprint and achieves that number of story points every sprint then it may be reasonable to ask whether that team is challenging itself or whether they might be sandbagging to ensure they always meet their commitments. Under no circumstances, however, it ever meaningful to use this or any other story point based measure be used across teams.

Quality of Output Metrics

Everybody tracks defects and they should. I will go into more discussion about defects in the chapter dedicated to that very subject. Comparing defects between teams, however, is not as simple as just tracking counts. If we knew where all the defects were in a product we could fix them before we released the product. The challenge is that we don't know where all the defects are or how many there are. Nor do we know that all the defects that have been seen have been reported. So, while we can know the number of defects that have been reported in a team's product that number is almost certainly different than the actual number of defects that are in the team's product. This makes using defect counts to measure the quality of a team's work products problematic and makes a comparison of one team's defect count to another team's defect count useless.

The same problem exists when looking at contained defects. Contained defects are a great thing but there is no reasonable way to reliably track them and putting mechanisms in place to capture and report on them is expensive and again, there is nothing actionable that can emerge from the exercise.

Metrics at the Individual Contributor level

Leaders are responsible for creating environments that allow the engineers on their teams to excel. An engineer who is being pressed to develop faster than they feel is appropriate is going to be forced to cut corners. It is not right to hold the individual responsible for a non-optimum output that is the result of him or her doing what their leader forced them to do. That is just one reason why it is a bad idea to use metrics at the individual contributor level. I was once approached by someone that had a look into our work tracking system who concluded, based on the numbers, that a particular engineer on a team was completely unproductive because over the previous several sprints the engineer in question had neither marked any defects as closed nor marked any stories as complete. Indeed, both assertions were correct but the conclusion the person was drawing was that the engineer was doing nothing productive when nothing could have been more incorrect. In fact, the engineer in question was a particularly good engineer who was spending most of his time assisting the other engineers on the team during a period when there were a number of difficult areas of the product the team was working on. The person best positioned to assess the engineer in question's contribution to the team was of course the engineering leader closest to the team. That person's assessment of the engineer was the exact opposite of what the pure numbers coming out of the work tracking system led someone else to assume.

It isn't just about the numbers though and certainly there are going to be engineers who are more proficient than others. The issue around metrics at the individual contributor level is that the individual contributor is only partially in control of his or her own destiny. A manager who cares more about quantity than quality will likely create an environment where it is not possible for an engineer to do everything he or she wants to do to prevent defects from leaking.

Why would you need IC Metrics anyway?

Most agile teams consist of between seven and nine individuals. There is usually an Engineering Leader responsible for the team. Most of the time the leader is responsible for one team but sometimes several teams. All engineering leaders have multiple responsibilities. Obviously, all leaders have to achieve their business outcomes but they also have two other equally important objectives; remove blockers that prevent their team from progressing and growing the careers of the people on their teams.

For that leader to do his or her job effectively they need to understand a lot more about what an engineer is doing than can ever be described in numbers. If a first level leader relies solely on numbers to evaluate whether an individual contributor is being effective or that first level leader can only express upward how effective the individuals on the team are using numbers then that first level leader is probably too detached to be effectively doing their job. They either need to be educated or replaced.

Metrics at the Engineering Leader Level

Using metrics at the Individual Contributor level is always wrong, using metrics at the Engineering Leader or Engineering Team level is appropriate and necessary if we are going to make the improvements we need. Engineering Managers must be held accountable for driving outcome improvements in both the quantity and quality of their outputs. Engineering leaders create the environments on their teams that enable their teams to succeed. The team should absolutely be aware of the objectives assigned to the engineering leaders but those objectives can never be directly cascaded to individual contributors. Engineering leaders must be given the responsibility and authority they need to meet their objectives and cannot simply be allowed to assign their exact goals to the individuals on their team.

Imagine a situation where a new leader has taken over a team that has a track record of an excessive amount of rework due predominately to large numbers of high priority defects being leaked. Because reducing the amount of rework would improve the team's efficiency and productivity it would be completely reasonable to set a goal for that engineering leader to reduce the amount of defect rework the team was engaged in. Assuming that the new engineering leader has been given the responsibility and authority to make the changes necessary to effect change then using the percent of rework metric to assess the new engineering manager is completely appropriate. Cascading the percent of rework goal or using that metric to assess any of the individual contributors on the team makes no sense because none of the individuals likely have the authority to make the changes needed to affect the outcome metric. Certainly, the leader needs to engage with the entire team and wants to share knowledge of the goal with everyone on the team but it needs to be done in a way that brings the team together to rally around the strategy the leader has to set to achieve the goal.

Engineering Productivity

Engineering leaders are successful if their teams are productive and continually improving. But what constitutes productivity and can we in fact measure it? This is the conundrum faced by all engineering leaders but it is one we have to confront.

Defining Productivity

The meaning of productivity in a software engineering environment is nebulous at best. Subjectively we can observe and compare teams and may conclude that one team is more productive than another but trying to apply an objective measurement to a team's productivity is something completely different. We can't simply take out a tape measure or a scale and measure any of the things we produce. We also have to be sure that any measure of productivity must also have a quality component. The idea that you can count anything as produced without factoring in whether it is in fact usable is obviously flawed. While creating software is not the same as manufacturing widgets it is easier to deal with the fact that you can't sell a broken widget than it is to deal with the fact that we are almost always releasing software that is less than perfect.

It is the responsibility of every engineering leader, or for that matter any leader, to make their teams as productive as possible and to improve both the quantity and the quality of the team's outputs over time. Leaders need to consistently ask their teams the 3 simple questions about both the quantity and the quality of their outputs:

1. Are we better now than we were?
2. Are we going to be better than we are now?
3. How do we know?

We need to find an answer to the **How do we know?** question. Because only then will we be able to objectively assess both the quantity and quality of our teams' outputs. The metric we choose also has to enable us to track improvement, and we need to ensure that the improvements are continuous. We need to

have measures that the team believes in and can rally around. Improvements cannot be made by the leader alone the entire team has to be involved in the process. The leader needs to create the environment that enables and encourages improvement but the team has to execute. Any measures we choose to assess and track progress must be measures that everyone on the team understands and trusts. They must be focused on results rather than on effort. They need to be things that can easily be gathered and not something folks on the team will argue about or try to game. Intuitively we want the metrics to address two dimensions:
1. How much was produced?
2. How good was what we produced?

While it sounds easy to ask the questions "How much did we produce?" and "How good was the thing we produced?" when it comes to software it is incredibly complicated. How much was produced is difficult because in a software environment we don't have a good way to define output. How good was the thing we produced is difficult because quality has many dimensions and the feedback loop is long and not particularly reliable. Nevertheless, in order to be able to assess our performance and progress we need to find a way to answer our **How do we know?** question. So, despite the difficulty of doing so we have to find a measure for outputs and our quality. If we do not have a method of measuring then other than optimism we have no way to know how well we are doing and whether or not we are getting better.

Measuring Outputs

Before we can measure anything, we need to know what it is that we are going to measure. This is perhaps the most fundamental problem we face while trying to measure outputs in the software engineering world. The simple to ask but difficult to answer question is "What output are we going to measure?". The idea that you can or should try to directly measure output at any level on a software project without simultaneously factoring in the quality of the outputs is certainly flawed and is almost guaranteed to drive the wrong behavior. It does us no good to manufacture 1000 widgets if 999 of them are defective.

We need to measure something, but we want the measures to be outcome focused and actionable. We want the measures to focus on results not on effort. We need to know what we are going to do with whatever measures we choose and to be able to set goals using the outcome metrics we select. Unfortunately, there is no direct output measure in a software environment that meets these objectives. I'm sure we all wish that there was but I'm sure we also understand that telling an engineer to write more lines of code is just not the answer to increasing productivity.

To understand why software outputs are not directly measurable think about the following. You are in a manufacturing context and want to measure the productivity of a person or team assembling widgets. It is easy to measure how many sellable widgets a person or team assembles in a given period of time. That is because:

- We know exactly what a widget is
- All widgets are identical
- We can identify almost all faulty widgets once they are assembled
- We know how to measure the time it takes to assemble the widget from beginning to end.
- We can easily calculate our Widget assembly success rate

When it comes to measuring software none of these process attributes exist. We don't know what code is going to look like when it is constructed, it is almost certainly something only developed once, it is not something that you can identify the beginning and end times of the activity for, it is next to impossible to immediately validate whether the developed code was correct or not and, while we can certainly measure the time an engineer spends coding a class method service or anything else, the actual coding time is usually only a small fraction of the time spent on designing, building and doing whatever local validations an engineer or team can accomplish before integrating with other system components.

To be sure, there have been as many failed attempts at measuring engineering productivity as there have been failed attempts at estimating project schedules. Lots of measures have been tried but to date none have emerged. There has even been considerable work done using estimated lines of code to predict project schedules. A prime example is Barry Boehm's **Software**

Engineering Economics which introduced the Constructive Cost Model (COCOMO) that was widely used on US Government and Department of Defense projects in the 80s and 90s. Certainly, the desire to measure outputs and the desire to improve project predictability are closely related and are fundamentally about making project schedule, scope and cost predictable.

The oldest and perhaps most meaningless productivity measure has to be lines of code. Two engineers developing the same functionality will almost certainly do so in ways that end up with different numbers of lines of code. And would we say the person who developed a solution using twice as many lines of code than the other person was twice as productive? I hope not because the number of lines of code, produced, while measurable has little to do with anything. Others have attempted to use techniques like function points or feature points but these are subjective and largely arbitrary. Today it is more common to look at story points as the unit of team productivity but while the unit being measured may have changed, the arbitrary nature of the unit of measure has not.

What all these units of measure share is that they are unscientific and arbitrary. As discussed earlier it is impossible to define what a story point is. You can't take a tape measure or scale and determine how many story points there are. Because the units are arbitrary measuring them in just about any context outside of looking at a specific team's backlog is meaningless. The practice of using a modified Fibonacci sequence when assigning points to stories adds to the challenge by the way it intentionally and I believe correctly removes specificity from the estimates. For these reasons, the we can only use the points that were estimated by any team within the context of that team.

Trying to look at story points across teams like referring to the number of units of a currency without identifying the currency. Surely nobody would be willing to exchange their Euros 1:1 for Indian Rupees but that is effectively what happens if we attempt to compare outputs based upon an arbitrary unit of measure.

The arbitrary and unscientific measures, while tempting, are also dangerous because they invariably are expressed in numbers and as we know, numbers almost always end up in spreadsheets. This often leads to people outside of the team, who may be very good with numbers but don't understand software development, using the numbers in ways for which they were not intended. A classic and prevalent misuse of any of these metrics is comparing teams or individuals to one another using any of these arbitrary measures. Imagine non-engineering management getting their hands on a spreadsheet that was showing the number of story points or lines of code that teams, or worse that individuals, were achieving per sprint and concluding that one team or individual was only half as productive as some other team or individual because they had only written half as many lines of code. Such data is readily available and easily accessible which does often lead to people drawing conclusions that are totally incorrect.

Imagine if we looked back at our widget factory and counted both the good and the faulty widgets in calculating the widget assembly success rate of the team or individual. The same danger exists when counting story points or lines of code. As foolish as this sounds, it happens all the time and almost always means someone having to spend countless hours attempting to explain the arbitrary nature of the measurements and why cross team or cross individual comparisons based on these types of measurements are meaningless. In the worst uses of these types of metrics some organizations have actually used these types of metrics when discussing the performance of individual contributors.

It is important to recognize that multiple people or teams, when given exactly the same problem to estimate are almost certain to arrive at different estimates for solving identical problems. This is true irrespective of the measure being used. It does not matter whether you are using story points, predicted number of lines of code that need to be developed, function points, feature points or anything else, the measure changes, the problem with the measures we have at our disposal does not.

I'm not sure who first said it but there is an old saying in the business that collecting metrics and collecting garbage are similar in that before you start collecting either of them you should know what you are going to do with them. This is absolutely true about wasting time trying to measure software development outputs. Lines of code per developer per day is exactly the kind of a metric that you can never do anything with. It does us no good to collect something unless it is going to help us improve of change our behavior. So, when it comes to measuring outputs we have to conclude that there is no objective direct measure available to us. The only thing that really counts is how much business value we are delivering and that is not something that is we know how to quantify.

Measuring Quality

Measuring quality presents a different but equally difficult set of challenges. It is relatively easy to say that we are going to measure quality by counting the number and severity of leaked defects found in the software we produce. The count and severity of leaked defects are often the objective measures used when assessing software product quality. For reasons we will discuss though, these measures may not be the right ones. This is not to say that there are not also subjective components to quality, there certainly are. However, measuring the subjective components is more difficult and not everyone will agree on the assessments.

Although defect numbers seem to provide an objective quality metric there are significant challenges with the leaked defect metric because:

- It can be hard to define what a defect is
- Not all defects get reported
- Not all defects are equal
- There is a long feedback loop

Unlike our widget manufacturing example where it was relatively easy to detect defective widgets at the point of manufacture, software is quite the opposite. It can be days months or years between the time software is written and the defects in the software are identified. Some leaked defects will certainly go undetected and others that are detected will never be reported. We do what we can to contain defects at the engineering team level and to identify and remediate as many defects as possible before we put it into the hands of our users but there is no team I know of that has never leaked a defect. So, at the point of construction we have to conclude that in addition to not having a good measure for the amount of output that was produced we also lack a good measure for the quality of what we are producing.

A further difference between widget manufacturing and software is that for the most part, once the widget has been sold it no longer has any costs associated with it. It is easy to track the cost of manufacturing and selling a widget. Software, on the other hand continues to cost, certainly in the form of maintenance and defect remediation, both of which we address through waste measurement, feedback and new stories, but more importantly there are on-going operational costs for hosting and operating the software. Even with the most defect free software imaginable the ongoing operational costs of the software are significant and present a real opportunity for software to have a significant bottom line impact

In the same way that we have challenges comparing story points across teams we face a similar albeit not so glaring problem when it comes to leaked defect data. Not all teams face equal challenges in their solutions and because live site defect data is very much a trailing metric more heavily trafficked areas of a product are much more likely to have customer reported defects than are the less trafficked ones or ones that are part of new product areas.

Another complication to simply using leaked defect counts is that the counts are far less important than the amount of time any defect takes to resolve. Some defects can be resolved in a relatively short period of time by a single engineer and others take considerable amounts of time and involve the work of multiple engineers.

What qualifies as a defect?

Any violation of the organization's Definition of Done encountered after the team has declared an item complete is a defect. Additionally, items that are not specifically identified in the Definition of Done but which cause high volumes of customer contacts are defects. Functional defects are relatively easy to recognize. Simply stated the software does something obviously wrong. Irrespective of the severity of the defect whether it is as serious as an exception being propagated to a user or a spelling error on a web page, it is obvious that what the user is seeing is a defect. Other types of defects are equally as serious even though the way they manifest themselves is not so obvious. Take for example the situation where a service performs poorly and so it is necessary to deploy additional computing resources to meet user demands causing operational costs to exceed what was planned? Or the situation where a less than ideal user experience is causing a large number of calls to a call center or in feedback to a help desk increasing support costs. Each of these situations and many more are equally impactful to the Total Cost of Operation for the system and so are legitimately also appropriately categorized as defects even though they are often not by most projects. It should be just as important to the business to fix a problem that causing increased costs as it should be to fix a problem that is causing an end user to see something happen that is obviously incorrect.

There can sometimes be a fine line between feedback and defects. Indeed, a user report that something is not working as advertised is both feedback and a defect but the key to the differentiation is the 'not working as advertised. Because Feedback is a good thing and defects are a bad thing we always want to be sure that we are categorizing and processing them appropriately. There are many ways to try and draw a line between feedback (the good kind) and defects. One way to think about feedback is to ask whether something is actually broken. Any feedback with the caveat 'it would be better if' is clearly feedback that is of the good kind. So too is feedback that begins with 'I would like it if'. Another way to think about how to differentiate is asking whether it is something that has to be done. If a feedback item is looked at by the product owner as a defect then it must be handled as such.

Not all defects get reported

Sometimes defects remain in a product indefinitely and never get reported. Nevertheless, they are still defects and may be harmful in not so obvious ways. Imagine a company name or contact information is misspelled. How embarrassing is it for a company to have its name spelled incorrectly on its own website? Yet such defects are at least imaginable and given that in multiple occasions I've had resumes cross my desk where candidates had misspelled the names of companies they had worked for it would suggest that such a defect is at least possible, or the possible situation where a contact email is incorrect on one page and correct on others it is entirely possible that the defect might never be found. These are definitely insignificant examples of defects that customers are not likely ever to report and which are also not likely to ever set off alerts. They are nevertheless defects and to some degree have the potential of having negative consequences to the company's reputation.

Not all defects are equal

It is easy to understand that defects vary in severity and impact. Some defects may be very serious in that they result in things like a complete inability to use the system, loss or corruption of data, security vulnerabilities or loss of revenue. Some defects can be in highly trafficked areas of a system while other defects may appear on rarely accessed pages. Obviously, a defect that results in loss of data or revenue is more significant than a spelling error on a web page. It is important that defects that do get reported get triaged rapidly and then addressed by the team as appropriate for the defect's assigned priority.

Perhaps the biggest inequality among defects is the effort needed to resolve them. Some defects can be resolved by a junior engineer in a matter of minutes or hours while others may require several senior members of the team working for days or even weeks to trace down and remediate some of the most challenging defects.

Defects aren't immediately reported

The amount of time that transpires between a defect being injected and that defect being discovered can vary from minutes to literally years. Defects that are found quickly are usually the most egregious or the ones located in the most highly trafficked areas of a system. There is usually a relationship between the seriousness of a defect the amount of time to discover but that is not always the case. We know that it is virtually impossible to test every possible situation and the more a piece of software is used the more likely it is that a situation will be encountered in the real world that was neither anticipated nor tested for during the normal development cycle.

Contained Defects

A contained defect is a defect that is **detected and resolved by an engineering team before a work item is declared complete.** Defects found by other teams such as internal testing teams are not contained defects. Every engineering team should have tools and practices in place to try to prevent defects ideally from being injected but certainly from being leaked. Practices and tools to support activities such as code reviews, automated static inspections and unit tests are some examples. Any time a defect is detected and resolved by the team before it declares a work item complete it is a good thing! That said, there is no outcome metric that can be defined relating to contained defects that is actionable.

While there are no reasonable outcome metrics relating to contained defects, the fact that any team is detecting and eliminating defects before declaring a work item complete as well as the method by which the defect was detected certainly has value. This is particularly valuable in an environment where CompStats are used. Tools such as SmartBear's Code Collaborator for code reviews and SonarQube for static code inspection will automatically capture some of this information. For activities such as unit testing and informal reviews if you choose to capture that information you will need to define a method and mechanism for capturing the information that is simple and relatively reliable.

Reframing the productivity discussion

Clearly in a software development environment we are challenged to directly measure either outputs or quality. At the same time, we need a way to assess and improve. We can't simply report back to project sponsors that we are making progress without being able to provide some meaningful metric. No leader I know wants to stand in front of a project steering committee or CFO and expect to get away with saying "trust me, everything is good and going to be better". What we need to do is to reframe the productivity discussion away from direct output and quality measures to a measure of efficiency. If we focus our teams on always working on the highest business value items and make our teams as efficient as they can be then our engineering organizations will be considered highly productive.

The outcome metric that we can calculate and report is the percent of available time teams are spending actually producing outputs. In other words, if we establish the right ecosystem we can use a single metric that encapsulates both the quantity and quality component of our outputs. This metric is the percent of time a team is spending on what I call **productive activities**. While this metric per se is neither a direct measure of quantity or quality it clearly represents how the team or organization are performing. With the right ecosystem in place it encapsulates both the quality and quantity dimensions of a team's output without using any arbitrary measures.

This measure has the advantage of being universally applicable to all engineering teams. It factors out the differences in team composition, engineering capability, number of hours worked per day or week, environments, complexity of the problem being solved and any other factor you might think of. It is easy to understand that any time a team spends being non-productive is taking away from their ability to be productive. If we can reduce the amount of non-productive time, which we will refer to as waste, on any team we will improve their productivity. So, it is correct to say from an engineering perspective the percent of productive time is the primary outcome metric we want to focus on. If we agree on that simple concept then we can state that for any engineering organization we want to continually increase the percent of time a team is being productive.

This is not to say that %ProductiveTime is a perfect metric[5]. It will take some time for any team to develop a baseline because when you start using this metric there will not be a baseline for waste. Establishing a baseline will take time but that is neither an obstacle to adopting the metric nor to beginning to focus on increasing the productive time of the teams. New projects or newly formed teams will also take time to establish baselines because until software developed by a team is in the hands of the user the amount of time being wasted resolving leaked defects will generally be less than it will be once the users start to get their hands on the software. In organizations where there are

---

[5] Obviously the question of whether the team is delivering business value is not captured in this metric but the decisions of what the team is working on are usually being driven from a product level.

independent testing teams there may be some defect resolution data available before software is in the hands of users. It is best to wait until the software has been used in production for at least the couple of Sprints and then declare your baseline. Even without an established baseline the actual number of hours being wasted on a team is an equally meaningful metric. Indeed, the number of wasted hours is an excellent starting point for moving in the direction of reframing the productivity discussion in the direction of waste.

A critical organizational requirement to being able to use %ProductiveTime as your outcome metric is ensuring that the team that owned the development of any portion of the product be the team that is responsible for also supporting the product once it is in production. This includes being responsible for fixing any defects found in the product. We also need to define and adhere to an SLA that specifies how teams are required to respond to defects and particularly to high priority defects found outside of the engineering team. When we have both the team owning end to end responsibility for the software and the priority based defect SLA in place then we will have the ecosystem we need. The E2E ownership and the defect SLA will have the effect of reducing a team's productive time by requiring them to divert resources to resolving quality problems in the software they produced. The defect SLA also aides us because it allows the team to delay working on low priority defects supporting the objective of ensuring that the team is always working on the items that deliver the highest business value.

If we are going to be measuring productivity by looking at the percentage of time a team is spending performing productive activities we have to find a way to calculate our productive time percentage. The formula we need to use is simple enough.

$$\%ProductiveTime = \frac{AvailableTime - WastedTime}{AvailableTime}$$

Figure 11 - The formula for calculating the percent of productive time is simple

By defining the productive time as a percentage it becomes possible to use the metric to answer the "how do we know?" of our three questions. Should we choose to do so, this metric also allows us to compare the performance of teams to one another. It is better to use percent rather than the absolute number of wasted hours as the outcome metric because it factors out items like team sizes, holidays, training, vacation times and any other items that make the absolute number of hours wasted potentially misleading. The metric also is clearly SMART and as we will address in the next chapter gas a large component that is within the control of the team. The absolute number of wasted hours, which of course has to be captured to calculate the percentage can also be used to put an actual cost value on the waste. At the project or organizational level the actual cost can be a very important item to highlight and one that may well be of interest to project sponsors[6] even if it is not the right outcome metric.

What we have to accept is that **the key to improving engineering productivity is the elimination of waste**. We also have to accept that the percent of waste is the metric that is the most actionable.

---

[6] It is not a good idea to make calculating the actual value too scientific. Best to use an average hourly rate no more granular than at the team or geography level

Waste

Waste is anything that takes away our opportunity to be productive. We can measure waste at both the team and organization levels. Waste is simply **the amount of time spent either performing non-productive activities or the time spent doing nothing because an engineer is blocked waiting for something to happen**. If, as an engineer you are fixing a defect you are engaged in rework. Re-work is a waste activity. Re-Factoring, in most cases is waste. If you are a Product Owner or engineer triaging a defect whether you decide you are going to fix it or not you are engaged in a waste activity. If you are an engineer refactoring code you are engaged in a waste activity. If you are an engineer waiting for a build to be deployed you are engaged in a waste activity. If you are a team or engineer waiting on a decision to be made by someone so that you can carry on with your work you are engaged in a waste activity. If you are an engineer investigating a production incident you are engaged in a waste activity. This is by no means a complete list of the activities that fall into the category of waste but they are examples of the types of activities that are not productive in nature and so they are waste because if you are engaged in any of them you are not being productive.

It is entirely legitimate to consider other activities such as meetings as part of waste because there are certainly cases where a lot of time is spent in useless meetings or where there are many people in meetings who are only there to listen. How you choose to define waste is not as important as recognizing that if you can get your teams to spend less time on non-productive activities then they will have more time to spend on activities that are productive. Most software engineering organizations are very bad at measuring waste. There are very few, in fact, that actively measure waste and even fewer actively involved in managing waste reduction. Those that do measure waste though often find that waste can sometimes exceed 50% of overall team capacity. The key takeaway is that any waste you can eliminate translates directly to additional productivity. Most organizations will be surprised to learn about the amount of waste they have within their organizations.

To be successful in any rolling out any change it is important to be transparent. This means being clear about what you are going to measure and what you are going to do with the data that you collect. It is also very important do not try and be overly exact in what you collect. The last thing you want to do is to create a collection process that ends up adding to the amount of waste you already have. It would, for example be disastrous to ever implement detailed time tracking so that waste could be tracked at a very granular level. The opportunity that a waste reduction program offers is significant and shining a light on it will almost certainly expose areas of "low hanging fruit" that can be addressed first.

Waste Collection First Steps

If you accept the assertions that waste negatively impacts any organization and that the less waste we have the more productive we are, then it is obvious that we need to do whatever we can to eliminate as much waste as possible. We need a strategy for our waste reduction efforts and that means identifying the first steps we are going to take. We want to start by identifying large buckets that every team on your project can agree upon and rally around. It is important to involve the engineering teams in the process of identifying waste buckets. Offer engineers to identify internal activities and processes that the engineers on the team see as waste but that may be imposed on them either by the organization or the engineering leaders. Be open to constructive conversations about whether such processes are indeed necessary and if not consider including those activities as waste buckets as well. Look for the instances of waste activities that are the most common and which have the most significant impact. For example, you will probably find that teams are sending significant amounts of time resolving leaked defects or supporting production operations. You might also find that your teams are spending lots of time waiting for software builds and deployments into test environments or as a result of turnover spending lots of time bringing new or replacement engineers onto the teams. As you identify waste buckets you want to group then into items that are owned by the teams and items that are owned by the organization. If you have independent testing teams you may find that teams are spending a lot of time waiting to learn where their defects are. It is neither necessary nor advisable to try to identify and track every minute being wasted as long as there are significant buckets to focus on. It also does not add a lot of value to try and be exact when measuring the impact of the items you identify. Some items may be easy to capture like the number of hours spent resolving the high priority defects that interrupt the team's iteration but for other items it might be easier and just as effective to assign estimated values to the most often occurring waste items and calculate the waste based on that average value. Work with members of your teams to come up with the numbers and encourage them to be as honest as possible with their estimates. It is important to keep the focus on the long term goal, which is reducing the amount of non-productive engineering time. It does us no real good to think about recovering wasted minutes when there are other areas where we are wasting days.

Figure 12 is an example of some of the waste activities worth documenting and samples of what the impact might be.

Waste Activity	Team or Organization	Average Waste Hours per occurrence
P1 Production defect	Team	32
P2 Production defect	Team	32
P3 Production defect	Team	16
Engineer Turnover	Organization	240
Broken Build	Team	8
Deploy Wait time	Organization	8
Awaiting a decision	Organization	40

Figure 12 - It is often easier to agree on a standard value for waste incidents and then assign that value to each of the occurrences than trying to capture actual values for the incidents.

It is easy to collect the number of hours an engineer spends resolving a defect but that is just the tip of the iceberg. The time spent recording the defect, triaging it, reproducing it, building and deploying it and then verifying that the defect has indeed been resolved are also contributors to the bucket of waste. To understand the full impact on engineering teams we need record time spent on these other supporting activities which are also waste are collected. For these items it is better to just estimate the additional efforts based on experience and just add that number of hours to each of the events.

The highest performing agile development teams are those that are always focusing on the highest business value and this is precisely the approach we want to take when improving our internal operations to drive down the percentage of waste. We do not need to capture and classify every minute of waste in order to start measuring and improving. Indeed, if we wanted to we could even begin by tracking the time being spent on the large buckets of waste and still have an outcome metric that is actionable. Any waste that is eliminated is going to result in improved productivity.

As with all metrics it is always critical to be transparent with why they are being collected and how they are going to be used to improve. This transparency is needed to drive accurate recording of the data you are collecting. It is also important that the definition of the metric be clear and unambiguous.

Investments to improve quality are not waste

Investments in quality are not considered waste and should be encouraged. Activities teams perform to ensure that they are not leaking defects need to be seen as productive because they are specifically directed at achieving the right outcomes. Developing unit tests, functional tests, performance tests, conducting code reviews or walk-throughs, correcting issues identified by static code scanners etc. are investments in quality. The effort expended by the team to remediate issues identified by any of the aforementioned, while not exactly productive in nature do reduce overall costs and so they too need to be considered as productive time. To some degree and from several perspectives this appears to be a contradiction but our ability to clearly delineate between activities prior to something being declared complete (story points banked) and something still under construction combined with the reality that a leaked defect is significantly costlier to remediate than one that is contained more than justify the distinction. It sometimes helps to think about the activities of containing defects as being similar to correcting the spelling mistakes in an email before you send it. To not make that distinction and to consider investments in quality to be waste does nothing to encourage the type of behavior we need to achieve the results we want. While we would all love to be able to hire engineers who always wrote perfect code that didn't need to ever be tested, the reality of the situation and the complexity of the systems we develop makes that an unreasonable expectation. We can't afford to make perfection be the enemy of progress.

Broadly speaking, waste falls into two categories, waste that a team creates and is responsible for reducing and waste that an organization creates and is responsible for reducing. Defects that the team leaks can't be fixed by the organization and organizational shortcomings cannot be corrected by an engineering team. A good way to begin your waste reduction initiative is to select buckets of waste that fall into each of these two categories to focus on. By doing so you have the opportunity to demonstrate to the teams that the organization is as committed to making improvements as you are asking the teams to be. Indeed, by creating these separate buckets you can also often create a positive competitive environment where the team and the organization are competing for the greater good.

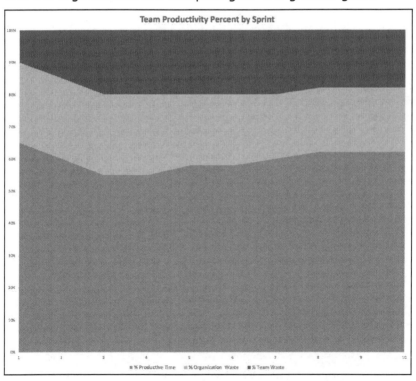

Figure 13 - The Percent of time a team spends doing productive work is the best outcome metric that relates to overall productivity available to us. Visualizing the amount of waste will help draw attention to the opportunity that exists

Waste for teams to address

Engineering teams need to address the waste that is created by their actions. Leaked defects and unnecessary refactoring are two of the most significant waste buckets found on most teams but there may be many more. Some of the team's internal practices may be seen by many engineers as waste and may need to be addressed. Items such as unnecessary meetings or meetings where everyone on the team is expected to attend even if they are not needed are examples of such waste. The primary team waste items, certainly defect resolution and refactoring are buckets that organizations serious about waste reduction need to consistently track.

Leaked Defects

The biggest single contributor to waste at the team level is normally rework. The most common cause of rework is leaked defects. A leaked defect is **any defect that is discovered after a work product is believed by the team to be development complete**. Any time that a team is working on any defect they are involved in a waste activity[7]. It is important to include the clause, <u>believed by the team to be development complete</u> rather than believed by the engineer to be complete because this recognizes the nature of the software development process in general, but the team processes in particular. Some leaked defects are so egregious that they require members of the team to interrupt what they are doing and immediately deal with them and they should. Other defects are serious enough to require teams to take them up as soon as there is a resource on the

---

[7] Low priority defects that have percolated to the top of the business value queues and which are committed to by the teams during iteration commitment are considered waste even though their inclusion in the iteration was planned.

team available, still others may just make their way into the backlog where they may eventually be resolved...or not. In any event though, remediating leaked defects is a major contributor to waste that only the team itself can address. The time spent resolving defects is waste irrespective of whether the defect created an interruption to the sprint or was included in the sprint through the planning phase.

One very bad strategy some organizations take to reduce team rework is to create a separate team to deal with leaked defects. While this might look like a reasonable strategy to some, what effectively happens is that the team that leaked the defects feels none of the consequences of the leaked defects. They are not interrupted to work on the defect, their velocity is not impacted and they miss the opportunity to learn how they might have prevented the defect from leaking in the first place. I like to use the formula below when thinking about how to drive change.

$$Change = Pain * Vision * FirstSteps$$

As the formula illustrates, the only way to effect change is to have the team feel the pain of leaking a defect, having a vision for where they want to be and to understand the first steps they are going to take to achieve the vision. If their leaked defects are resolved by another team then there is no motivation for the team to change its processes to improve the quality of their outputs. By forcing the team to take responsibility for their own defects and resolve them appropriately the team feels the consequences because they see a drop in their velocity and potentially by missing their sprint commitments. So, the pain is clearly present as is the vision of improved velocity and fewer asynchronous interruptions. The first steps will be up to the team but they must be directed at improving quality and are best left up to the team to select.

Broken Builds

Broken builds are another common waste area for teams to address. It is unlikely that a team will ever get to the point where a build never breaks. The nature of the software development process means there are always going to be broken builds. Waste relating to broken builds is created when more than one engineer is impacted by the break. If a broken build impacts only a single engineer then it needs to be considered a normal part of the development process. When a build breakage impacts multiple engineers then a waste event is created.

Refactoring

While it may be considered by some to be controversial to categorize refactoring as a type of waste there is certainly an argument to be made that if code needs to be refactored then it was not done correctly in the first place. Now some proponents of Test Driven Development have made the case that refactoring is a natural consequence of the process of getting code to pass a test and then cleaning up that code. In fact, in this circumstance the refactoring is not something that should be considered waste because, assuming the refactoring is happening prior to the code being declared complete (points banked) then it is not rework as much as it is a normal step in the development process.

Refactoring does become waste if it is needed for any reason after points have been banked. Many will disagree with this position because they will point out that what they are doing is either making the code more efficient or making it more reusable or maybe just restructuring it. While it may be good to refactor for any of the aforementioned reasons, the fact remains that the engineers doing the refactoring are not doing anything that is productive therefore the refactoring falls into our definition of waste.

One argument often used to defend refactoring as not a waste activity is that requirements can change over time and that it sometimes makes sense to enhance a service or method to perform additional functions rather than to create a specific method to perform the newly identified function. There may indeed be situations where this is true, however, there are other circumstances where the argument is not correct. Organizations need to decide where they stand on this when they define their waste categories. There is often a balance between delivering what is needed today and looking at the long term.

To illustrate the challenge, I recall once being told we needed to develop a monthly billing service for a subscription offering. I objected arguing that what we needed was a temporal billing service that would allow us to bill for any period and perhaps to cover other billing models as well. We went on to build a service that would allow for any calendar period to be used for billing and to leave the other possible billing options out as they were unlikely in our business. So we went out and developed the service that supported billing at the day, week, month or yearly period. By doing so we looked at our business model and decided that any other model really made no sense. The cost of developing the multiple models was a little higher than just developing the monthly model but with a small amount of effort we provided the business with a new set of billing options that they could use if and when they wanted to. Had we chosen to develop just the monthly billing service and the business later decided they needed one or more of the other models then we would have had to find a time on the backlog to do the work and then on the engineering side decide to either to modify the monthly service, clone and change it or refactor the code to handle the additional models.

Production Support

Teams need to have E2E responsibility for their products. Part of that responsibility includes providing what is generally called Level 3 support when there are production issues. Level 3 support requires someone from the team to immediately address production issues. Whether the support results in actual software changes or whether it is because of another reason it is important that we look at the need to get the engineering team get involved means that there was a flaw somewhere that, if the software were either more resilient or autonomic could have avoided the need for the engineering team to engage.

Feedback is not waste

High performing agile teams develop in increments and iterations and continuously incorporate user feedback in their products. They want to get features in front of users as soon as they are viable so they can learn, respond and improve. User feedback is what helps drive the improvements. The team or Product Owner who believes they can predict and develop exactly what their user community needs is either fooling itself or developing for a community of one, themselves. User feedback is not the same as a defect. The distinction between feedback and defects is not always entirely clear. We want and need feedback. Not taking feedback is the equivalent of not listening to users and can never be seen as waste.

Planning is not Waste

As hard as it is to believe there are actually people who believe that if an engineer is not coding he is not being productive. There are also folks who believe that the sooner an engineer begins to actually write code the sooner he or she will be complete. Neither of these beliefs are based in reality. As discussed earlier in our widget example, it is impossible in a software development environment to determine exactly when work on a particular method or class begins and there are no discreet milestones that are observable. Engineers spend considerable amounts of time planning how they are going to structure and write their code and to an outside observer this may appear unproductive but it is. Indeed, the engineer who spends more time preparing and understanding the problem they are trying to solve and even goes beyond to think about how they can build their software to be more deal with just the problem immediately in front of them is probably taking actions that will avoid later rework and refactoring, both of which are waste activities.

Another area of planning activity that is not waste is anything that is being done to prepare for future sprints. Participating in any of the pre-commitment activities are investments in the productivity of the team and as such are not waste.

Training is not waste

It should go without saying but training is not waste. That is true whether the training relates to technology training or any compliance training an organization may require. There are probably instances where engineers will identify certain mandatory organizational training as waste and in some cases they may be correct, however, that is an issue that needs be dealt with in another context.

Waste for organizations to address

Every organization wants to get the most out of their teams. Because all teams are different and all problems we solve are different organizations have a responsibility to do everything they can to enable their teams to be as productive as possible. We all want to be able to staff our teams with 10x engineers but as we all know that is unlikely to be possible and even if it is possible we would want to provide those 10x engineers an environment where they can be as productive as possible. This means getting teams as close as possible to the point where everything they are doing is productive and waste is eliminated. This seems easy enough to understand but it is a lot harder to get into practice. Organizations need to be willing to invest to provide the environment that reduces waste.

Every organization is going to have a different set of waste buckets. Ask each of your teams to identify and prioritize the waste buckets they feel are the most impacting. Consider asking teams the simple open question "What slows you down?" and considering any answer you get as a potential waste bucket. There is a lot to be gained by having the teams see that leadership acknowledges and prioritizes eliminating the waste they are responsible for as well. Here you want to look beyond just the engineering teams and include whatever other teams you have in your organization as well. If you have an independent testing team or DevOps team it is entirely possible that you can identify additional waste reduction activities in those areas as well. Some of the most common and some often overlooked waste items that are shared are discussed in the paragraphs below but this is by no means an exhaustive list.

Hardware

Many organizations fail to recognize the impact on productivity that poor performing hardware has on their engineering productivity. In most organizations the single most scarce resource are engineers themselves yet some organizations fail to properly equip their engineers with the fastest most powerful hardware available. It isn't necessary to provide every engineer with the latest and greatest hardware but multiple core machines with large SSD drives, multiple high quality displays and as many GB of memory as can fit in the machine should be the minimum every engineer is given.

Tools not bought but being paid for anyway

As in the case of hardware, engineers also need to be provided with the tools they need to do their jobs. These tools cost money and organizations have budgets, however, the failure of an organization to provide its engineering teams with the tools they need in sufficient quantities to eliminate waste usually results in the organization paying the far greater than what it would cost to buy or license a tool. The opportunity cost of not providing the tool may not show up in direct spending but does in either poorer quality or lost productivity[8].

Tools you build when you could buy

Many organizations believe that some of their tooling requirements are so unique that the only way to satisfy their requirements is for them to build the tools themselves. There are few cases I have come across where that is actually the case. While it is true that the products an organization develops are unique the tools they need to build and operate the products rarely are. This is even more true in the new world of open source where large communities of developers have banded together to construct and continually improve the tools they need to do their jobs. If an organization decides to build tools to satisfy their "unique requirements" then the engineering time used to construct, test and maintain the homegrown tools needs to be tracked either as waste or as some other category of work because in all but the rarest of cases time spent on such tools

[8] If you are putting a value on the waste as discussed in the section on Reporting Waste

does consume engineering effort that is not being spent on developing product that can directly benefit the business.

Build and deployment

Many organizations have products that take significant time to build and deploy. The shorter the feedback loop the more productive the engineer can be. Large projects can often have build and deployment times that stretch into hours once integrations begin. Automated testing in Continuous Integration pipelines can also significantly add to the amount of time it takes to get code from the engineer into an integration environment. This is not in any way to say that we don't want to have a strong set of automated tests but we do want to be measuring and monitoring the amount of time needed to execute the full suite of tests, particularly when they are part of an integration pipeline and, doing whatever is possible to reduce the time needed to test. While it is unlikely that an engineer would do nothing while a build and deployment is occurring, organizations that fail to invest adequately in constructing highly automated continuous integration and deployment pipelines missing an opportunity to shorten their cycle times. Where there is a lack of automation in the pipeline or when deployments become an issue it may become necessary to engage engineers to fix problems which, from the perspective of the engineering team is a waste event. This category of waste is organizational because it is the organization that has to choose to make the investment to automate the pipeline not individual teams.

Virus Checkers

We all want our environments to be secure. That means we want to be protecting ourselves and virus checkers are one of the tools we use to do that. However, virus checkers also are very compute intensive and when they are configured incorrectly they can have a significant negative impact on any activity that involves moving files or data from one location to another or even in some instances can impact compile times.

Environment issues

I have yet to see an organization where every team did not want to have their own production class environment. Environments are expensive though and the expense is not just what you are paying Amazon, Microsoft or some other cloud provider for your servers and capacity. Until an organization reaches the point where environments are available on demand more environments generally means more DevOps personnel and they almost always mean more cost.

Communication Bandwidth

It is becoming more common for teams and organizations to be geographically distributed. While communication tools have improved significantly it can still be problematic when teams are dispersed and insufficient bandwidth can make communications difficult. Meetings that are impacted by poor communications usually take longer than meetings in person. The additional time spent in meetings due to insufficient or unreliable bandwidth is waste.

Excessive Planning

Asking teams to engage in excessive planning activities is a waste activity. If we are always focusing on delivering the highest business value items then it stands to reason that attempting to size work that may never actually be done is a waste activity. Teams need to focus on ensuring that they always have an adequate backlog and that the items of highest business value are the items that they focus on. Teams need to work closely with product owners and functional specialists to maintain a backlog that is roughly two or three iterations worth of effort to ensure that they can avoid getting into a situation where they are forced to work on low value items for lack of adequate high value items to commit to for an iteration.

Defense of Diagnostic Metrics

In several places I have pointed out that because lots of engineering activities generate metrics and that these metrics often find their way into spreadsheets. These spreadsheets can become the subject of meetings where conclusions and assertions are made that need the involvement of one or more team members to discuss and sometimes defend the metrics. With the exception of CompStat meetings where the purpose is learning the time engineers spend in such meetings is a waste activity.

Analyzing non-actionable Metrics

At several points I have mentioned that there is a tendency to take any number, plug it into a spreadsheet and start to analyze it. Once that cycle starts there is a strong possibility that the metric is going to start to be used to compare teams to one another. This can create a culture where a lot of time has to be invested by members of the team justifying or refuting claims that result from the analysis. Generally, this means that the teams themselves end up getting involved in defending what is more likely than not some diagnostic metric or arbitrary metric. I'm sure many people can relate to having participated in discussions where they had to explain over and over again that the team banking the most story points or writing the most lines of code is not necessarily the most productive.

Decision Making

Having an engineering team lay idle or be constrained to doing low business value activities while they wait for a decision is often a significant contributor to waste on engineering teams. Sometimes teams try to compensate for being blocked by the lack of a decision by taking up other activities like deciding to resolve open low priority defects. When this happens there are two consequences, first of all the team ends up not working on the highest business value items and secondly when teams are working on defects that is seen as team waste. It is more important to capture the amount of waste than it is to properly categorize it but it is worth noting that the cause of the waste was a blockage that was created by the organization and not by the team.

Unnecessary Meetings or attendance at meetings

It will come as no surprise to anyone that most projects have a lot of meetings. Meetings are not necessarily bad things and are needed to ensure decisions are made and communicated. Unfortunately though, in most cases once a meeting has been put onto a calendar it is unlikely to be shortened and if a recurring meeting ever to be cancelled. Adding to the waste potential is the fact that there are often more attendees in meetings than there are participants in the meeting.

Constant Interruptions

The majority of engineering teams today are located in open workspaces and cubicles. While these environments are conducive to collaboration they are not necessarily the best environments for allowing engineers to concentrate. While it is impossible to quantify the impact of noise and other interruptions on engineers it is worth casually monitoring the situation to observe whether the interruptions become excessive and acting to reduce the frequency of interruptions and reduce the level of unnecessary noise and traffic through the engineering team areas.

As mentioned earlier it is not uncommon to have organizations create tiger teams of tap engineering resources to work on particularly challenging problems. It is perfectly understandable to take these actions but the impact on the team needs to be considered. While it is difficult to measure the impact of taking the best resources from the team to work on special projects there is certainly an impact on the team and while the absence of any particular resource or resources from the team is not waste per se, the impact of the asynchronous interruption is at least worth monitoring and possibly worth assigning an actual value to such disruptions/

Personnel Changes

When members of an engineering team need to be replaced, or the decision is made to increase the size of a team a significant waste event occurs. When new members need to be brought onto the team the existing members of the team will need to invest time interviewing potential new members and then in training activities to bring that new person up to speed. The hours spent by engineers on the team in the replacement process are all waste[9].

Personnel turnover falls into two categories, regretted attrition and non-regretted attrition. Regretted attrition includes situations where an individual chooses to leave the project on their own accord and, as implied by the name of the category, has a negative impact on the organization.

Regretted Attrition

Regretted attrition is an organizational waste category. It is an organizational category because it is largely beyond the ability of the team or first level engineering leader to be able to make the kinds of changes needed to attract and retain top talent. High levels of turnover are extremely destructive to a team's productivity as it necessitates training new engineers on the team processes and on the team's code base. Turnover does not have to be just replacing engineers who are leaving a team, it also applies to situations where new engineers are being added to a team. Even in those cases where engineers are being moved between teams there will be some impact for new engineers to familiarize themselves with the new team's code base. There will also almost always be some learning curve associated with new engineers at the very least coming up to speed with the domain the team is working in. Getting new engineers up to speed usually requires the most experienced people on the team to stop what they are doing to educate the new team members. The most experienced people on the team are also typically the ones who are involved in the interviewing and recruiting of potential new employees and while this is

---

[9] Just for the sake of clarity in the case of an engineer leaving the team the absence of that engineer is a reduction in engineering capacity not a waste event.

absolutely a necessary and valuable activity, when it is caused by turnover the engineering team's contribution is a waste activity that needs to be counted. When looking at the impact of turnover on the team it is important to factor in both the time it takes for a new engineer to come up to speed but also to count the loss of productivity of the folks who have to train the new team members. It is virtually impossible to put an exact value on the waste created by turnover or adding engineers to the team but the value is significant and should not be underestimated. The waste is not measured in hours or days, it is measured in at least weeks but probably months.

Non-Regretted Attrition

Non-regretted attrition includes all personnel turnover that for one reason or another was directed by the organization. Generally this includes situations where people are either managed out of the organization for performance reasons or where people are transferred to other projects for the good of the overall organization. The impact of non-regretted turnover to the engineering team is not any different than regretted turnover, however, because in both of these situations the organization ultimately benefits from the turnover it is best to not consider non-regrettable attrition as waste. Non-regrettable attrition is more appropriately dealt with by treating the incident as a reduction in capacity rather than as waste.

Environment for Improvement

If you accept the assertion that the primary outcome all engineering organizations can focus on is increasing the percentage of time they working on productive activities, the next thing to do is to look at how you can best organize and execute to improve that outcome. This involves creating an ecosystem and organization designed to identify and reduce waste and friction. There are organizational attributes that are important and there are processes that need to be implemented as well.

I have consistently made the point that pain is a necessary component of the change process. The best way to create this pain is to have highly motivated teams that are committed to becoming more productive and by requiring those teams to accept responsibility for providing production support and resolving high priority defects that appear in their software. By having teams asynchronously absorb the full consequences of the problems that they introduced can we expect them to feel the pain, learn and improve. We need to be transparent with all of the data related to our outcome metrics and use the data in a positive manner. Organizational leaders need to publicly state their policies regarding metrics and outcomes and need to adhere to those policies.

The Organization Paradigm Shift

From an engineering perspective it is easy to see that waste is an objective outcome metric. From the larger organization perspective though the change means that they have to adopt an entirely new paradigm with respect to their software development investments. It is a total departure from the decades long pursuit of being able to predict when a project is going to be done and how much it is going to cost. It would be a mistake to underestimate the complexity of the organizational challenges that may be faced in adopting this new approach.

The importance of creating a compelling business case to support the paradigm shift can not be overstated. An engineering organization is unlikely to be able to sell such a major change using "trust us" as the key selling point. This is, after all a change management issue and as always when we think about driving change we need to reflect on the formula for successfully driving change:

Change = Pain * Vision * FirstSteps

The Pain

As with driving any change we first need to establish a reason for making the change which I refer to as the pain. In this case the pain that is the catalyst for the change is the amount of waste that the organization is incurring. An accounting of the amount of waste within the organization such as that shown in Figure 13 showing just how much waste there is in the organization combined with an identification of the largest waste buckets of the particular organization will provide the basis of what needs to be a compelling description of the problem. In the process of building the case it may prove valuable to put an actual monetary value on the waste.

The Vision

Intuitivaly the long term vision would be the elimination of waste. But as we all know it is not going to be possible to eliminate all waste. To ensure that the organization understands that the total elimination of waste is neither achievable nor desireable it is best to think about the concept of Total Cost of Quality to help identify the optimum point for your organization. Total Cost of Quality is explained below but for the purpose of creating our case for change we will always be able to say that the vision component of change formula can be satisfied by achieving the lowest total cost of quality.

Understanding Total Cost of Quality

Total Cost of Quality is a concept that emerged from the Six Sigma world. Total Cost of Quality (TCOQ) is comprised of two components. A **Cost of Quality** component, (COQ) which is the amount spent to ensure a product has the right amount of quality, and a **Cost of Poor Quality** component, (COPQ) which is the amount you spend or lose because your product has less than perfect quality. Understanding how your TCOQ is distributed can be a great help in deciding how to best allocate resources between the two components. As discussed earlier, perfect quality is not something we are normally looking for. The time and expense of trying to achieve perfect quality are astronomical and there is no real way to determine when that perfect quality has been achieved. It is hard to believe that we would ever be able to release a product or feature if perfect quality was a prerequisite to releasing. Because perfect quality is not the objective we have to accept that there will always be costs associated with accepting that less than perfect quality. We want to know what those costs are if we are to be able to choose where we need to invest. At the same time we do need to have sufficient quality to keep customers happy and to keep production costs under control.

The idea behind TCOQ is that there is an optimum point for every system. That no quality has an infinite cost because it would be impossible to use a product that had no quality and perfect quality also has an infinite cost. Details of the concepts around Total Cost of Quality can be found in most books that deal with Six Sigma including "The Six Sigma Handbook" by Tom Pyzdek. From our perspective though it is sufficient to understand where projects are on the curve. Everyone can decide where their optimum point in the curve is but from our perspective it is about knowing where we are on the continuum.

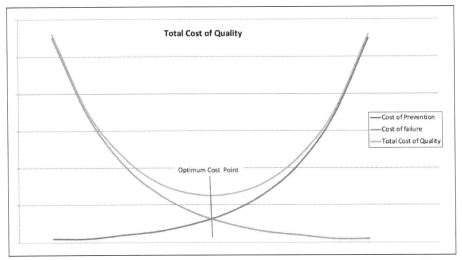

Figure 29 – The Total Cost of Quality is the sum of prevention costs and failure costs. The secret is in getting the balance right which is what the optimum cost point illustrates

Cost of Quality

Costs of Quality are the investments you make to enable the delivery of a quality product. Any expenditures made to deliver quality are considered costs of quality. For the purpose of simplicity, efforts by engineering to deliver quality such as time spent developing unit tests or performing code reviews are best considered integral parts of the development process rather than as costs of quality. Engineering leadership's proximity and familiarity with the internal ongoings of the teams combined with the feedback loop created by the defect SLA and leaked defects provide adequate information to determine whether the right balance is being struck on the teams.

Cost of Poor Quality

Costs of poor quality are all of the costs we incur because our product is not of perfect quality. Many of the costs of poor quality are difficult to directly measure and need to be estimated. Even though we are not striving to achieve perfect quality we still need to consider that the costs we incur because our products are not perfect are still components of the cost of poor quality.

Many of the costs of poor quality have to be estimated. For example, it is impossible to estimate the impact that poor net promoter scores have on the ability to sell new products.

Activity	COQ	COPQ	Collected
Defect resolution		X	Waste collection process
"How do I?" support calls		X	Call center data
Testing costs	X		HR data on team size and costs
Refunds and cancellations		X	Sales data
Tools for engineering	X		Actual costs
Training for engineers	X		Actual costs
Poor Net Promoter scores		X	Imputed

Figure 30 - There are many components that contribute to Total Cost of Quality in a Software environment. Some examples are in the table above

The First Steps

Deciding where to focus your initial waste reduction initiatives will depend on the data you gather from your organization. Whatever they are though there will always be some preparation involved. Those steps are independent of whatever the initial reduction targets are and are discussed below.

Establish E2E Ownership

I once took over a project that was moving a segment leading product onto the cloud. One of the first meetings I attended was to discuss the subject of escalations. The meeting was kicked off by a colleague who announced that the objective of the meeting was to determine how we were going to staff the escalations team. This was going to be the team responsible for fixing production problems. I ended the meeting quickly by saying that there would be no escalation team because the teams that leaked the defects were going to be the teams that had to fix them. I pointed out that if the team that was leaking defects wasn't being impacted by the defects that they had leaked that a key component of the change management formula, namely the pain component, that it would be much more difficult to drive whatever improvements were needed. I will reiterate that for change to occur there must be some pain being felt.

End to End product accountability is the first thing that must be established to reduce waste and improve the productivity of a project. Establishing End to End responsibility and ownership makes it clear to the team that they are not done with any work product when they declare code complete or even when code has moved to production. Teams need to understand that they are responsible for supporting the products they produce for as long as those products are in use and that the responsibility means they are going to have to comply with the organization's defect SLA and provide support for production issues.

High Priority Defects

High Priority defects need to be dealt with by engineering teams expeditiously whenever they occur. The priority definitions established by the organization will determine which defects teams need to address immediately and which they can take up either as soon as a resource on the team becomes available or in subsequent sprints.

Production Support

It is important to be explicit about the production circumstances under which we expect teams to provide. The best way to define the expectations is to align the support in terms of Service Level Agreements. When it comes to defects it is relatively straight forward to define a defect SLA dictating how a team is going to respond to the various defect priorities. When it comes to Production support differences in organization structures and responsibilities may make it a little less clear but the ITIL Support tiers provide a solid framework for defining at what point an engineering team needs to engage on production related incidents. Generally engineering teams need to engage when an ITIL Tier 3 event occurs and remain engaged until the issue has either been resolved or lowered in severity.

Staffing and Organizing

Every organization is going to be different but there are guiding principles that are known to improve performance and there are also things that need to be avoided. It goes without saying that we always want to staff our organizations and in particular our engineering teams with the most skilled people possible. Yes, we would all like to say that we are only going to staff our engineering teams with the proverbial 10x developers but that is not a very achievable target. What we can achieve is to staff teams with skilled engineers who work well together and who exemplify the right values. We need a mix of engineers who have different levels of experience ranging from interns and recent university graduates up to very senior and experienced engineers and sometimes architects. In many organizations there is a need to also create cross project or cross organizational teams that support multiple engineering teams. Obviously, no organization consists purely of engineers and we also want to staff all of the other roles with the most qualified personnel we can find. Figure 14 shows a typical project organization chart

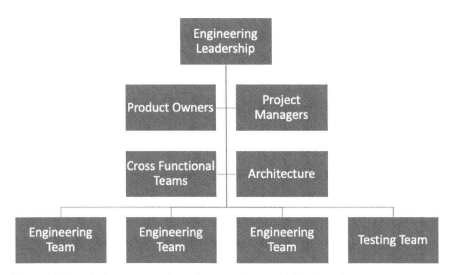

Figure 14 A typical project team for agile projects has multiple engineering teams, an independent testing team, cross-functional teams, project managers and product owners.

To the greatest extent possible we want our engineering teams to include all of the resources they need to function as independent organizations. At the same time we need to recognize that not everyone can be expert at everything and that there are some functions within the system development domain that require levels of expertise and specialization that make putting people with some of these highly specialized and skilled people on every team is not the right thing to do for either the teams or the specialists. We need to reach the point where teams can be fully accountable and responsible for completing the work they commit to in an iteration without being dependent on support for any resource outside of their control. We address these highly specialized functions and removing the dependencies on them by ensuring that all of the dependencies that do exist on these specialized resources are resolved before any stories are committed to.

Engineering Leadership

Engineering leaders need to be both leaders and managers. To be a successful leader they need to be looked up to by the team and need to have a strong engineering background. Engineering leaders do not need to be able to do all of the work being done by the team but they do need to have enough technical expertise to be able to thoroughly comprehend what the team does and be able to add technical value. They also need to be managers and have a responsibility to develop the careers of the members of their teams. This means that leaders have to become competent coaches. Becoming a competent coach requires becoming a good listener and leading people to conclusions not just providing a solution. Engineers are trained to solve problems so it can sometimes be difficult for new engineering managers to make the transition from solution provider to coach.

Figure 15 - The best coaches lead people to a conclusion through an iterative process of inquiry

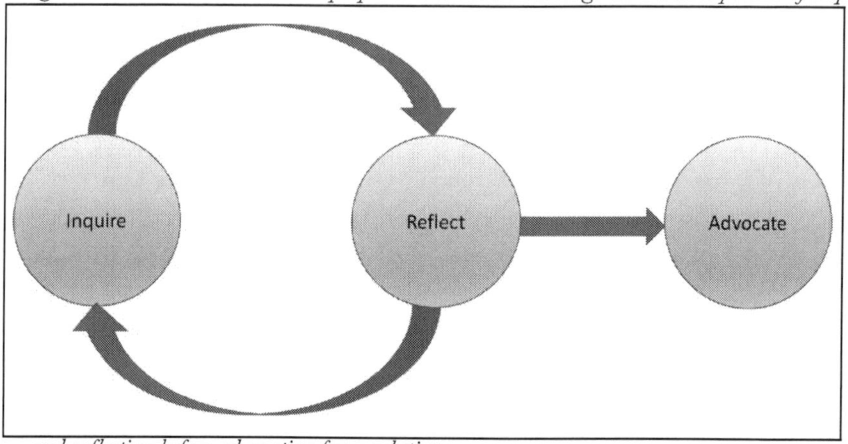

```
    Inquire  ⟷  Reflect  →  Advocate
```

and reflection before advocating for a solution

One of the biggest challenges faced by engineers who change career paths into management is dealing with people. Engineers are motivated and trained to solve problems but they are also trained to believe that problems can be solved. Software engineers learn to write code that assesses a situation, makes a decision and then executes some action. Given the same situation the code will make the same decision and the same instructions will be executed. Dealing with people is nothing like writing code. The number of variables involved when dealing with individuals far exceeds the number of variables any engineer faces when writing code so any thought that every problem that looks like one seen in the past can be solved by the same solution is likely flawed.

if you look across the software engineering organizations today it's very common to see the best engineers moved into management roles. Usually what happens is a vacancy becomes available and so we look around and we choose the best engineer and offer that engineer the opportunity to move into a management capacity. Sometimes that best engineer on your team may not want to become a manager but may feel compelled to take the position because they see it as career progression. The best engineers do not necessarily turn out to be our best engineering leaders but when we move our best engineers into engineering leadership we do in fact lose the best engineers on our teams.

Providing people career growth paths is one way to help motivate and retain them. At the same time we want to provide the growth path that aligns with their personal goals. Nobody wins if our best engineers feel that the only path they have to grow is by moving into management. We need to provide parallel growth paths for managers and engineers and not pressure engineers to move into management to gain what they might perceive as the only way to advance. When considering transitioning any engineer into an engineering management role we have a responsibility to be clear about what the transition involves. It is important to be explicit that the change is a career path change and that once in the new role if they continue doing their old job that they won't be doing their new job.

Engineering

Engineering teams are typically comprised no more than seven engineers with nine being the top end. While there will almost always be a mix of skills and experience on the team it should always be the case that anyone on the team is generally capable of working on any story in the team's backlog. Everyone on the team and who attends the daily stand-ups and other ceremonies needs to be a pig[10]. There are no chickens on engineering teams. There will almost certainly be folks on the team with different skills who for the most part need to be capable of filling in for each other. The notable exception to the rule is the role of

---

[10] The pig and chicken metaphor refers to an old fable of unknown origin used to describe the difference between commitment and involvement. The Pigs who are totally committed and the chickens who are only involved. Another way to think about it is in the context of breakfast where the pig has to sacrifice himself to provide the bacon but the chicken just has to lay the egg.

the Product Owner who in most cases is not an engineer. Whether the Product Owner is a part of the team within the organization's reporting structure is not important as long as both the team and the product owner understand that one cannot succeed without the other and that they will either fail or succeed together. The Scrum master is another specialized role on the team. The Scrum master role is best filled by an engineer on the team who has received additional training in the responsibilities of the role.

Noticeably and I believe necessarily absent from the engineering team are the roles of project manager and of tester. They are absent for different but equally significant reasons which are discussed below. I have stressed at a number of points how important it is for teams to have End-To-End responsibility for their products and for responsibility and accountability to be handed out in equal doses. There are places for both project managers and testers on projects but neither have roles on the actual engineering teams.

It may not seem intuitive but having testers on engineering teams does not improve quality. Let me reiterate that. **Testers on engineering teams do not improve quality**. This holds true whether we are discussing traditional testers or specific engineers on teams whose job it is to test or write automated tests. The so called Software Development Engineer (SDET) may have a role on external testing teams but having them actually on the teams creates the same over the wall problem that we have when we have traditional testers on the engineering team. Having testers on teams may mean fewer defects leaking from the teams but that is very different than saying testers improve quality. Testing is a necessary component of any quality strategy but if any team's quality strategy is testing alone then that team does not have a serious quality strategy. Having testers on teams creates what can be described as an internal "over the wall" event where engineers write code and then pass it to someone else to test.

It is easy to be concerned about the consequences of not having testers on teams. If the only thing we did was to move testers off of engineering teams and onto teams of testers then that concern would be born out. What we have to do is be clear about our expectations for engineers to deliver quality software and to be clear about the consequences of not achieving that level. I recall a conversation with Mark Carges, who at the time was the CTO at eBay on the topic of engineering mindset. Mark was lamenting the quality of some of the engineering practices in the organization and described a continuum where there were engineers on one side of the spectrum who completed coding and turned to the testers and said "tell me where my defects are" and on the other side were engineers who when they completed their work and turned it over said "I dare you to find a defect in my code". We need to move more of our developers to the I dare you to find a defect in my code side.

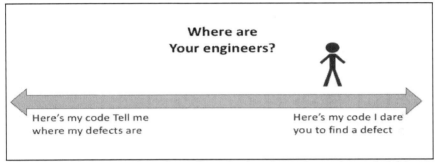

Figure 16 - Engineers need to take quality seriously and not rely on others to find defects in their code

Some will argue that engineers are not well suited to testing their code or that engineers do not have the skills or mindset needed to properly test code. This is an interesting argument and one that is often heard from both testers and engineers. These arguments can lead to self-fulfilling prophecy but there is no reason why this needs to be the case. Developers are normally very good at testing their code for the so called "happy paths", in other words in testing code they write to prove that it works. But our expectations have to change.

One of the common consequences of having Testers on Teams is the emergence of hardening sprints. Hardening sprints become necessary when the backlog of "development complete" stories reaches the point where the testers on the team can no longer keep up and so the entire team has to stop developing and help the testers complete testing of the "development complete" stories. Hardening sprints are nothing more than a costly consequence of a code and fix mentality. They are a clear indication that the team either has been operating with an inadequate Definition of Done, or that they have not been meeting the criteria specified in their Definition of Done. In any event, any time there is the need for a hardening sprint it is a clear indication that the team is operating more in a Serial Waterfall model than in an agile model.

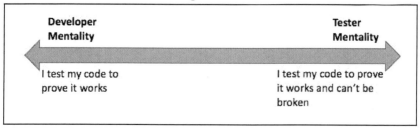

Figure 17 - Developers need to do a better job at thoroughly testing their code and not just looking at the happy paths.

In any event, most organizations choose to have an independent testing function external to the engineering teams. It makes perfect sense to have these organizations but it is important that the expectation is set that the external team not be expected to find a majority of defects but rather that they focus on end-to-end functionality and that any defect they found be considered a leaked defect which engineering teams deal with as if they had been found by customers. The engineering teams are solely responsible for ensuring that their work products meet all of the criteria laid out in the project's Definition of Done. Every engineer on the team needs to understand that basic requirement and every engineering leader has a responsibility to make sure that the team executes accordingly.

Cross Functional Groups

Most projects will have cross functional teams that support all of the engineering teams. Some specialized areas such as user experience, architecture, database engineering and user interface design require specialized skills that may not reasonably or efficiently be placed on the engineering teams. End to End testing is another example of a team that may have cross team responsibilities, however, e2e testing differs from other functional areas because it is a function that generally engages after the engineering teams believe their work is complete while the other cross functional teams do most of their work before the engineering teams can begin the actual construction of their components.

Architecture

Architects play a critical role in every engineering environment. They have many responsibilities with perhaps the most important being the definition of the technical boundaries between the many functional areas of systems. Architects also are key to selecting and driving the selection of new technologies that teams are going to use in their specific areas. The most successful organizations I have seen are those who distribute their architects throughout the teams and appoint a chief architect who maintains overall responsibility for the architecture and matrix manages the distributed architects. The distributed architect model has the advantage of having the architects being closer to the engineering teams and brings with it the advantage that the architects for each of the areas becomes a pig rather than being seen as a chicken.

Project Management

Project Managers play a critical role on any large project but need to be kept outside of the engineering teams. There are many places where project managers provide significant value to projects and the organization. Project managers are skilled at planning, tracking, staffing and reporting. They are very skilled at keeping track of every detail of a project and ensuring actions are taken to resolve issues and keep projects on track. On software projects there is a tremendous amount of data available about what is happening throughout the development environment. Many project managers are drawn toward numbers and are comfortable analyzing the numbers that they collect. Most of the numbers that are available are diagnostic in nature and the correlation between those numbers and the outcomes we are trying to achieve are weak at best and coincidental at worst. Traditional project management techniques to fix schedule and quality issues such as adding engineers to a project to accelerate it or adding testers to it to improve quality are almost never the right answer.

One of the best books ever written about managing software projects is **The Mythical Man-Month** by Fred Brooks. The book is amazing as it was written over 40 years ago and many of the problems the book addresses are the same problems many projects experience today. It is the epitome of the 'experience is inevitable, learning is not' syndrome. One of the key points made in the book is that <u>people and time are not interchangeable</u>. This is a concept that project managers often seem to reject. I have yet to meet a project manager who has been able to fully deal with this reality. Engineering leaders on the other hand recognize this reality and understand that you cannot just throw resources at a problem to shorten a schedule. In the book, which was initially published in 1970, Brooks describes many of the challenges large and complex software projects face and does an excellent job of explaining why adding people to a project to speed things up has exactly the opposite impact. Yet to this day there are no doubt thousands of project managers, and to be honest a lot of engineering managers as well, who believe adding engineers to a project that is behind schedule will help accelerate a project. Adding resources to a project more often than not has the exact opposite consequence.

Nearly as destructive as the belief that adding resources to a team can accelerate progress is the belief resources can be shifted between teams to accelerate progress. Indeed, in most cases moving people between teams is less destructive than simply adding people to a project because the tools and processes on a project are usually the same on all teams working on a project so the learning curve for engineers moving between teams is normally a lot shallower than for folks joining from outside the project.

A further manifestation of the project manager's attempt to interchange people and time is the approach to overtime. There is nothing wrong with asking teams to work overtime, indeed it is rare that over the course of a project that it would not at some time be needed. Most teams willingly absorb requests to work overtime. This is different though than putting numbers into a spreadsheet and calculating that if everyone on the project worked an additional 10 or 20 percent per week that a corresponding acceleration in the project schedule would follow.

Projects that include software development are notoriously difficult to plan and execute. Whether you look at it from the perspective of cost, schedule, scope or quality there are challenges and simply too many unknowns that are inevitably going to surface. Project managers, by nature and role will want to engage in a quixotic quest to find a solution for one or more of any project's unpredictable dimensions. By allowing project managers to interfere in the operations of the engineering teams we run the risk that they will begin to direct the teams which is not the role they should be taking. The agile manifesto calls for responding to change over following a plan which is not the DNA of project managers. What we have to do is to ensure that that project managers are engaged in activities that are assisting the engineering teams rather than trying to control the engineering teams. Project managers should never be allowed to attend agile ceremonies such as iteration planning sessions or daily stand-ups. In agile teams scrum masters and product owners, not project managers, are responsible for planning and scheduling the work of the engineering teams.

While there are many things we do not want project managers to be doing there are an equal number of items we do want and need them to be doing.

Testing

Before any organization releases a product or feature to its customers some level of testing needs to occur. Engineering teams need to be accountable for delivering quality and need to feel the consequences of failing to do so. When testers are placed on engineering teams much of the responsibility for quality shifts from the engineers to the testers. We have all probably been in a situation where a leaked defect is found in production and the first question asked is "Why didn't testing catch that?". On teams that include testers it is common and appropriate to see teams at least internally start to track the progress of development with the states of "development complete" and "test complete". When engineering teams contain testers, it is common to see engineers start focusing more on writing code rather than developing and validating their own code. This can lead to backlogs of code written by engineers that needs to be tested by other members of the team. There is a tendency to look at the backlog of items needing to be tested as items to be tested and not as **items that need to be tested and which almost certainly contain a significant number of**

defects. These defects will ultimately need to be resolved and retested before any of the stories that had been in the "development complete" state can actually be completed. It is not at all uncommon to see these backlogs turn into the need for testing sprints or hardening sprints where teams have to pause developing new functionality to focus on cleaning up the mess left behind from previous sprints. Testers have a role on the project but they are best organizationally placed outside of the engineering teams.

Testing teams are most effective when they are external to engineering and organizationally treated as if they are users. Any defect identified by a testing team needs to be treated as a leaked defect and dealt with using the same SLA as that used for production. Testing organizations have to act as a final safety net protecting the company from releasing a product with serious defects. They need to focus on end-to-end functionality and may also perform exploratory testing.

Some organizations will at least partially staff testing teams with Software Development Engineers in Test (SDET). SDETS are software engineers who are in the role usually developing automated tests.

Those who advocate for a mix of testers and engineers on agile teams generally do so either because they believe developers aren't capable of testing their own code or because they believe developers are too expensive to have them spending their time testing code. Those who argue that developers are not capable of testing their own code often point to what I refer to as the developer mentality which leads them to test their code to prove that it works while testers allegedly have the mentality and are trained to test code to both prove that it does what it is supposed to do and also that it cannot be broken. This argument is a favorite of Quality Assurance Managers and there is certainly some truth to the categorization of the mindsets. There is, however, no reason why software engineers cannot or should not be held to a higher bar when it comes to delivering quality. There is no reason why a developer is not capable of thoroughly validating their own code and proving that it cannot be broken. Indeed, there is no reason why engineering leaders should not hold engineers accountable for doing just that. On the other side there are those who contend that developers are too scarce and expensive a resource to have them spend their time testing code. Anyone making that argument is failing to understand the costs they are incurring when defects bounce between developers and testers.

Injecting testers onto teams creates an over the wall situation on teams that if not managed can lead to a 'code and fix' mentality among developers. This occurs when a developer finishes coding, maybe does some fundamental testing and then turns their code over to the testers to find defects. Teams that have testers embedded on them will often insert states in their workflows or on their Kanban boards called Development Complete and Testing Complete. Creating these two distinct states, while necessary usually lead to a number of negative consequences including hardening sprints.

Measuring the effectiveness of testing teams is challenging and there is no really good metric available. It is easy to identify the diagnostic metrics that should never be used but difficult to find an outcome metric that should be. The one measure that seems to work best is the percentage of defects leaked from engineering that are discovered by testing. If we break the product cycle into phases and measure leakage from engineering to testing and from testing to production it is easy to calculate the effectiveness of testing. In the same way that a perfect engineering team would never leak a defect, a perfect testing team would catch every defect. While this may be the best way to measure the effectiveness of testing teams there are problems. First of all the metric is not exactly SMART because it is at least partially dependent on how well the engineering teams are doing at containing and eliminating defects before they declare their work products complete. The second problem is that we know that defects can live in products for a long time before they are discovered and that some defects never get reported.

Figure 18 - Measuring defect leakage at each handover point is likely the best metric for measuring the effectiveness of test teams.

If you still want testers on teams

Some organizations will no doubt choose to keep testers on engineering teams. In those cases, it is just as important that the waste created by rework on the team be measured. Any time that testers on the team have nothing to test it is also a waste situation. This means shining a light on the amount of rework that is occurring on the teams. The easiest way to do this is by using whatever work flow management tool you have to have both a development complete and a test complete state in your workflow. The extra state can then be used to create a queue for the internal testers and to move stories between the development and testing states. Organizations that have testers on teams need to closely track the size of the queue of stories in the testing queue and the rate of recidivism they are observing on the teams. They also need to ensure that any defects found by testers are recorded in the defect tracking system and that any time spent by engineers resolving those defects is recorded as waste. They are also advised to treat defects found by testers on the team with the same SLA that is used for defects that have leaked from the team.

Monitoring the queue of stories in the development complete state is important because if the queue of stories to be tested gets too large the team begins to run the risk that the queue will grow to the point where it becomes necessary to stop development and have the entire team focus on testing or even to the point where a hardening sprint becomes necessary. When the queue of stories to be tested backs up the normal reaction is to stop development and assign the engineers on the team to testing. This is of course ironic because the reason often given for retaining testers on teams is that engineers don't have the right skills or mindset to effectively test.

It is also important to ensure that when production support incidents or high priority defects occur once the team has released a component that the team avoid the temptation of asking one of the testers to deal with the incident rather than assigning the person on the team who is best qualified to quickly resolve the issue.

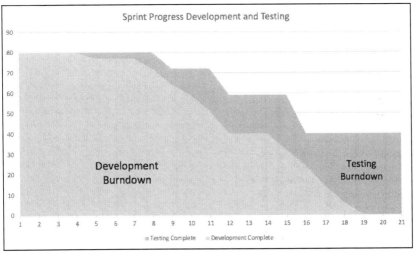

Figure 19 - With Testers on teams it is important to track the progress of the stories as they move through the process so that it does not become necessary to insert a hardening sprint.

Hardening Sprints

One of the common consequences of having Testers on Teams is the emergence of hardening sprints. Hardening sprints become necessary when the backlog of "development complete" stories reaches the point where the testers on the team can no longer keep up and so the entire team has to stop developing and help the testers complete testing of the "development complete" stories. Hardening sprints are nothing more than a costly consequence of a code and fix mentality.

Hardening sprints are a clear indication that the team either has been operating with an inadequate Definition of Done, or that they have not been meeting the criteria specified in their Definition of Done. In any event, if a team or project has a hardening sprint somewhere in their plan it is a clear sign that the team is operating more in a Serial Waterfall model than in an agile model. It may not be every project's goal to achieve Continuous Delivery but hardening sprints have no place in a continuous delivery model.

The illusion that more is done than is Done

Whenever the word complete is used in a workflow state it tends to lead folks to believe that something is actually complete. For example, when there are states for Development Complete and Testing Complete it is not at all uncommon to see a backup of the testing work queue. This creates the illusion that if testing could be sped up that the product or release could go live sooner. This is an illusion because it fails to address the amount of development work remaining to fix whatever defects the testing will discover.

We need our teams to develop the mindset that Development Complete means Ready for Live Site. Another negative consequence of having testers on the teams is that as with any other over the wall activity it creates an illusion of progress when in fact there may be none. Anyone who has worked as a software engineer knows that just because something compiles doesn't mean it is going to work. Indeed, in many cases when there is any concept of Development Complete and Testing Complete as part of the development within a Scrum team or within a Kanban flow what is really happening is that the team is accumulating technical debt associated with defects that are likely to be found and will need to be resolved before the feature can be released. There is an illusion created that work is done when it is not. This often leads to events such as hardening sprints or testing sprints and ultimately moves the project execution model away from agile and toward serial waterfall.

Other than the regulatory situations mentioned earlier, any organization that is on the path to Continuous Delivery has no need for teams of testers. The only exception is when a new product is being developed and there are not yet any users. In these cases up until the product has been built to the point of it being viable at the macro level, a team of testers can play a valuable role acting as users.

Testing does not improve engineering quality it highlights the absence of engineering quality.

The Waste Management Process

As development organizations the most significant improvement we can make is to reduce the amount of waste we are incurring. Hopefully by now you are convinced that this is true. But eliminating waste is not going to just happen. Every organization stands to benefit greatly by reducing waste but that is not going to happen without making some investments. To be successful, organizations need to commit to actually running their waste reduction initiatives as an actual project. This means assigning a manager to the project to ensure that the project is planned and tracked. It will not take a large team but there will be investments that need to be made.

Identify waste buckets

Earlier when the topic of waste was introduced a number of common and possible waste buckets were identified. No two organizations are identical though so the first step is to identify the buckets that your organization has. Also, as discussed previously you need to classify your waste as either team waste or organizational waste.

Allocate buckets to teams and organization

Every waste bucket identified is going to belong to either the overall organization or the engineering teams. Each waste bucket needs to be allocated to one of these two groups so that the progress of each group can be tracked.

Define Standard Waste Values

It is not going to be possible to know exactly how much waste certain events will generate. Personnel turnover is an example of such an event. We know that there is significant waste created when an individual leaves a team and needs to be replaced. We know that the impact is significant but we do not know exactly what the impact is. Rather than trying to record the actual impact of each of the turnover events it is better to just agree on a value and assign that value to each of the events that fall into that category. In this particular case, since the engineering teams are the ones being impacted by turnovers and it is best to let the teams agree on an average and then adopt that number.

Create Collection Mechanisms

In order to calculate the percentage of waste we need to have mechanisms to capture both the hours that are available in an iteration and the hours that are wasted. It isn't necessary to make a make a major investment in developing these collection mechanisms but it is necessary to have whatever is developed be easy to access, transparent and reliable. Good reporting is also necessary because being able to visualize the status and progress of the initiative will be critical to the success of the initiative. Spreadsheets can at least initially be adequate for collecting the data but as the program progresses and visibility increases it will be better to develop a simple internal facing web application to collect and report on the initiative. Scrum Masters are probably best positioned to collect waste data.

Begin Collecting Waste data

As soon as team and organizational waste buckets are identified and the collection mechanism is created the process of collecting waste data can begin. It will take time to develop a baseline but as the data is being gathered it can certainly be shared and publicized. Waste can be captured and shared with the teams and the organization as soon as the waste collection mechanism can be created. It will only be possible to begin reporting on the percentage of waste once iterations have completed but it will certainly be possible and valuable to begin displaying the absolute number of wasted hours as they are recorded.

Managing the waste collection process and reporting is one of many examples of where a project manager can significantly contribute to the project.

Establish Improvement Targets

Once baselines for waste are established it makes sense to establish targets for waste reduction. Targets should be created for both the organization waste category and the team waste category. Achieving the team reduction targets are the responsibility of the engineering team leaders, achieving the organizational waste reduction targets is the responsibility of the overall project leader.

Prioritize Improvement Initiatives

Most teams and organizations will be surprised to learn just how much waste they have. It is not uncommon to find instances where waste approaches and even exceeds 50% of the team's capacity. Eliminating any waste is good but when organizations see the extent of waste they have and see the opportunity that eliminating the waste offers there can be a tendency to go all in to eliminate it. What we need to do is to approach waste elimination in the same way that we approach our product backlogs, by focusing on those items that provide the highest business value which in this case is going to be the waste buckets that are the highest sources of waste and not trying to work concurrently on all of the waste areas.

Reporting Waste

Our outcome metric is clearly the percent of team productive time. To calculate the percentage we need to sum the amount of team and organizational waste incurred over the reporting period and to track the data over time. Because transparency is vital it also makes perfect sense to publicize a categorization of the accumulated waste and the amount of waste for each of the buckets being tracked. At the very minimum it makes sense to report the categorization at the team and organization levels but there is no harm in reporting at each level it is being collected. Reporting this data upward helps to drive accountability and has the positive consequence of sharing the responsibility between the team and the organization. It is also entire reasonable to assign actual costs to the waste buckets. Most organizations have average hourly rates for what employees cost and it makes perfect sense to use this figure to calculate the actual costs. Putting actual costs on the waste is a valuable tool for getting executive level support for making improvements, particularly those improvements that relate to the organizational waste buckets.

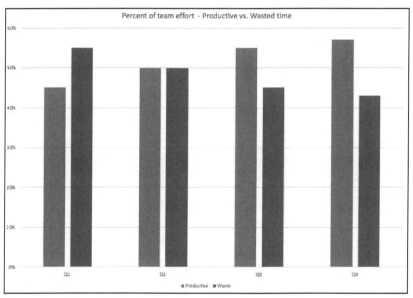

Figure 20 – A graphic showing the amount of spend on productive activity vs. waste activities provides a compelling picture of how efficient the project is executing.

It will never be possible to eliminate all of the waste in an organization. Waste reduction targets need to be reasonable and SMART[11]. Once baselines have been established it will be

[11] SMART – Specific Measurable Attainable Realistic and Time-Boxed

possible to track improvements. Assuming you are assigning costs to the waste means you will also be able to track the amount of cost that has been avoided due to improvement initiatives. It is perfectly reasonable to celebrate milestones when target saving amounts have been achieved. It is motivational to celebrate these milestones at both for organization and team level. It is important to recognize that eliminating waste is something that will benefit every portion of the organization. Waste is generated by all areas of the organization and all parts of the organization have a role in its elimination. The waste data can be shared and it is perfectly legitimate to slice, dice and analyze the waste data in any way the organization sees fit. Unlike many of the numbers that are available throughout software development, waste is something that is based on something that is not arbitrary. If during a quarter an organization loses 2000 hours of productivity and the average employee cost is $150/hour, the cost of that waste would have been $300,000. That is real money that could have been spent producing something useful had the waste not been incurred.

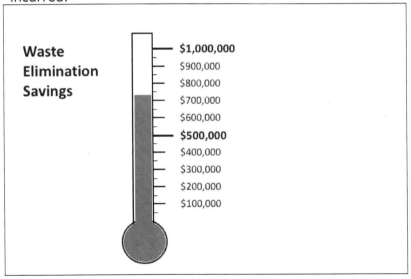

Figure 21 - A Goal Progress thermometer prominently displayed can prove to be a very effective motivational tool which can be used at all layers of the organization

Being able to publicize the savings from any initiative is a great thing. It is even better that as the team is able to spend more time on productive activities their output of high business value items will increase at approximately the same rate that waste is being reduced. While the putting an actual value on the savings is highly motivational, the calculation of the actual savings is not likely to be exact. To augment the estimated savings data, it is a good idea to also publish the trends of the various waste activities not as monetary values but as counts of events.

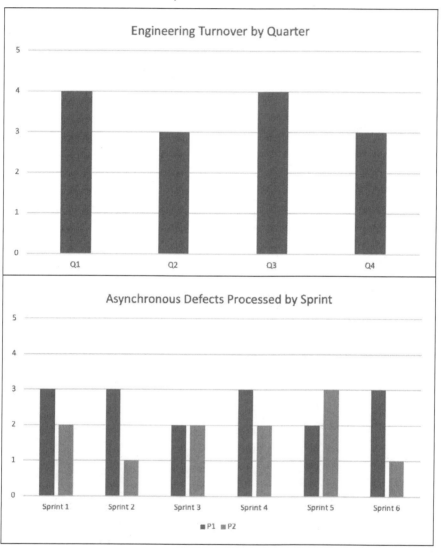

Figure 22 - Publishing waste event data such as in the above charts is not as motivational as the monetary saving but it is more accurate and also important

Reducing Waste

Every organization is going to identify their own set of waste buckets and prioritize their waste reduction items differently. Their primary focus is going to be on reducing waste within our engineering teams because they are the most constrained and expensive resources. The most common waste area for all organizations is likely to be the amount of waste caused by leaked defects. This makes defect management a very important subject to address. The most obvious way to reduce this waste is to leak fewer defects. The way to accomplish that is to improve the quality of the products engineering is creating.

Organizations need to provide teams with the tools they need to improve empower them to decide how to improve and hold lengineering leadership accountable for improvements. It is important for organizations to create a positive environment that makes progress transparent and celebrates successes. At the same time we must create an ecosystem that makes teams feel the consequences of leaking defects, particularly high priority defects. In parallel, organizations have to do what they can to reduce waste in the areas where they are responsible for creating the waste.

This directly means we need to have our engineering Foremost among them are items related to quality, the management of defects that do escape and the amount of time it takes for software to get from the engineer's workstation to the production environment.

We need to focus on managing quality which means we need to understand what quality means to the organization. We need to express that definition of what quality means and express that meaning in our Definition of Done. We also need to define the processes that are going to be followed for defects that do leak from the engineering teams.

Managing Quality

All organizations want to achieve a high level of quality in their products. A high level of quality is not the same as perfect quality. Organizations need to understand what the right levels of quality are for their products and more granularly for specific areas of their products. They also need to understand that there are multiple aspects of quality and that usability is also a critical attribute that needs to be looked at as a quality issue. Recognizing these needs is critical to defining quality objectives and developing the appropriate quality strategies to achieve those objectives. Organizations need to develop and maintain comprehensive Definitions of Done addressing all of the quality attributes and put a Service Level Agreement (SLA) in place to ensure teams respond to leaked defects as specified in the SLA. They need to set the expectation that the engineering teams are responsible for product quality for the life of the product and that before any work product is declared complete it has to meet the criteria identified in the Definition of Done.

The systems we build today are complex. Most are comprised of numerous services that together perform all of the functions needed to accomplish whatever your system does. Many systems also integrate open source components supported by communities of developers. Some even interface with systems of external providers to accomplish critical business functions. Generally, engineering teams are responsible for a set of services which they will have written or imported and which are consumed by other teams. The engineering teams providing services and products are responsible for the quality of the components they developed. The teams must ensure that any interfaces to services they call or invoke are thoroughly validated. It is the team's responsibility to determine how to validate what they deliver. Once made available whatever was produced will be consumed by any other service or function which goes through whatever authentication and authorization is in place. Teams need to understand that once something is made available, **consumers are not only going to use the component or product as envisioned, they are going to use it however they want to use it**. Under any circumstances though, the scope of validation for any team developing a service is generally confined to what they specifically develop and consume. Even with the most comprehensive Definition of Done in place and validated against, it is probably too much to ask any team to validate the use of a service they are delivering in every end-to-end context that the service can be utilized. What teams can do is to thoroughly validate that their services function correctly and that they can consistently deliver the level of service their consumers expect and deserve. The end to end validation of business functions that consume sets of services to accomplish their objectives often makes the creation of independent testing teams necessary. That said, engineering teams must adopt the mindset that **Development Complete means Ready for Live Site**.

Some organizations have invested in Continuous Delivery systems that are so reliable and fast that they can afford some failures because when they do occur they can quickly be fixed. Even in those cases, however, there will usually be areas in products where they can not afford major failures. In such cases extensive and thorough testing will always be necessary. Test automation can be used to accomplish some testing but test automation itself is software that takes time and costs money to develop and is also susceptible to defects. Additionally, any test automation developed at the UI level is both time consuming and notoriously expensive to maintain. So while test automation plays an important role in any quality strategy it is by no means the single solution to ensuring quality. The fact that we are looking at agile developments makes test automation at the UI level even more complicated as we expect things to change over time which makes significant UI automation almost impossible to achieve.

The solution to delivering software with fewer defects is not by getting really good at testing, rather it is by having engineering leaders driving a quality mindset into their teams and by developing a mindset on the team that has them feeling upset at themselves every time a defect is found. Rather than thinking about the handoff to an end to end testing team as a transition from development to testing they need to think about it as a release of their product into production. It is up to engineering leadership to eliminate anything that fosters a "develop then test" mentality. When independent testing teams find a defect they need to be treated exactly as if it had been found in production.

In any of the "these people develop and those people test" models there is a specific hand off of a work product to another person or team to validate someone else's work. When a handoff occurs there should be no expectation that defects are going to be found. While it is a good practice to have engineers review each other's work, any formal handoff of what would be an incomplete work product creates a **development** phase and a **validation** phase which is an "over the wall" event. Setting clear expectations that the validation event is not intended to find defects and treating any defect found that is best avoided but at the very least needs to be managed. The environment engineering leaders create for their teams needs to be designed to contain as many defects as possible before the product is declared complete.

Managing quality is not easy but by pushing the right mindset into the teams, creating a comprehensive and living Definition of Done and creating and enforcing an SLA that holds teams accountable for not delivering the level of quality required it can be achieved.

Definition of Done

Traditionally most projects have developed release criteria that defined the level of quality needing to be achieved before software could be released. This often led to very long testing cycles during which numerous defects were usually found and remediated leading to either target release dates slipping, release scope being reduced or quality bars being redefined. In the most egregious cases defect backlogs have been scrubbed to lower the severities or priorities of defects so that the backlogs fell below the agreed upon release thresholds. One of the key reasons we moved to agile is to be able to release software regularly as soon as it is complete. Completion needs to be defined though and that is done through the creation and adoption of a Definition of Done. Every agile project needs to develop its own Definition of Done. Easily said, not so easily done. The Definition of Done contains a list of what it means for any piece of work to be complete or as I like to say, done-done or ready for live site. In an agile world this translates to a list of items that must be validated before a team can either bank story points or if using Kanban move the story to the complete column. Under any circumstances the term complete or done-done if you prefer, means that the work artifact is believed to be ready to be made available to users with no further development or validation.

It is vital that the Definition of Done address both the functional and non-functional attributes of your software. It is obvious that the primary functional requirement of any Definition of Done is that the software do what it is supposed to do but that is just the beginning. Performance, reliability, scalability, supportability, security and maintainability are just some of the non-functional attributes that also need to be validated. Concurrently it is important to be realistic when executing against your Definition of Done. Without getting overly complex it is important to consider that there are always going to be situations where it makes sense to decide not to do something that is included in your Definition of Done. This is more often the case in non-functional Definition of Done space than in the functional area. For example, work that is being done in seldom trafficked or non-revenue producing areas might not require performance or characterization testing it probably still requires security and penetration validation. It is the responsibility of the engineering manager to ensure that the items in the Definition of Done are validated by the team before declaring any story complete. Any violations of the Definition of Done that are found downstream need to be handled as defects using the same SLA as defined for production items.

While it sounds easy to create a Definition of Done it can actually be quite difficult. Some of the difficulty is the challenge of striking a balance between including everything that you can think about adding to the list with and keeping the list of items brief enough so that the teams developing the software can relate to the list. The other big challenge in developing a Definition of Done is the reality that at the story level most of the non-functional items in a Definition of Done are not easily validated. It is a good practice to review the items on your Definition of Done and ask whether each of them, if not completed will constitute a defect when discovered in production. If there are items your Definition of Done requires that can either never be detected in production or if detected would not result in a defect then those items do not belong in your Definition of Done.

Much of the complexity in developing a Definition of Done derives from the incremental nature of agile development where features are developed and ideally delivered incrementally over a series of sprints or perhaps continually. Most features are comprised of multiple stories and it is rare to be able to find a situation where each and every single story comprising a feature can be released to production as soon as it has been completed. As discussed earlier, the more common model is that sets of stories comprise release components that get released together. There are also often times where features, being developed by other teams, are dependent on one another.

There are certain non-negotiable items that have to always be part of any Definition of Done, actually implementing the story, security and performance being the most obvious, but other items in a Definition of Done can be more challenging, particularly when looking at individual stories. The idea that we would be able to conduct performance characterization testing or penetration testing at the story level is neither reasonable nor economically sustainable. That said, considering a story to be complete when subsequent validation might identify problems that need resolution before release means that we run the risk of accumulating technical debt. This is particularly true for non-functional requirements that may not always be seen by product owners as being as important as functionality. We all understand that technical debt is something we need to avoid. We also understand that prioritizing the cleaning up of technical debt ahead of developing additional features is often difficult because the technical debt is less visible to product owners than the need for additional functionality. Therein lies a dilemma we face in incremental delivery and thus with determining how best to execute against your definition of done. As illustrated in Figure 23, features are delivered as sets of stories. Some number of those stories are necessary for the feature to be viable. In other words, until you have completed all of the stories needed for viability (illustrated in the green shaded features above the horizontal lines) you will not be able to release the feature at all. The same holds true once the point of viability for a feature has been achieved, in that it is rare that you would be able to release at the granularity of each and every story. It is more likely that you will release sets of stories that I like to call Release Components.

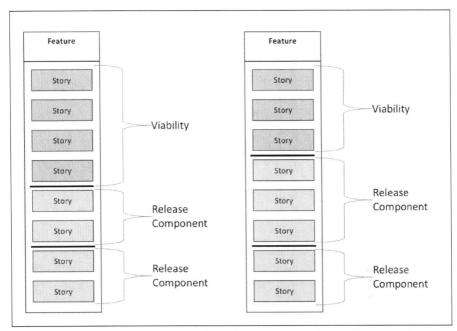

Figure 23 - Striking the appropriate balance about when we need to avoid accumulating technical debt can be critical to how your Definition of Done is perceived

Keeping in mind the fact that from the business perspective the highest performing agile teams are the ones that are always working on the highest business value items, it follows that once a feature has been declared viable and released to users that the team may well move on to items that are of a higher business value than the next set of stories in that feature's backlog. In the most extreme circumstances they may pause or even stop development of that feature altogether. We never want to be in the situation where the software being used has only been validated from a functional perspective.

Because it is virtually impossible to validate all of the non-functional items in your Definition of Done for every story, we have to develop a strategy that allows us to complete stories without losing track of the accumulating technical debt that comes with not validating that the non-functional attributes of the story have been completed. The accumulation of technical debt creates an environment where if not carefully managed can lead the project into serial waterfall.

Many organizations choose to address the impracticality of validating every story against every Definition of Done criteria is by developing separate Definitions of Done for stories and releases[12]. The intent of the multiple Definitions of Done is to allow teams to move on to the next story once a story has only been validated against a story level subset of the completion criteria. While it is completely understandable to take this approach, it creates a situation where a story has been labeled as complete but will only be ready for production after it is validated against the release subset of the Definitions of Done as well. This allows the team to bank the points and show progress on their burn down chart when in fact there is still work to do that is not reflected anywhere. This increases the probability that a project will slip into a serial waterfall execution model where within a sprint or over a series of sprints, stories that are believed to be complete and had their points banked and reflected in burn down charts are actually not complete.

In fact, what will be happening is that there will be an increasing backlog of technical debt accruing, potentially over multiple sprints. This may eventually end up requiring one or more sprints to clean up the technical debt remaining from previous sprints before software can be released. It is very easy for the technical debt to accumulate under the radar. Among other things this raises questions about the truthfulness of burn down charts and overall project status. There are two things we can do to avoid the serial waterfall trap:

1. Make Technical Debt Transparent
2. Restrict Technical Debt Growth

Make Technical Debt Transparent

There are several strategies to avoid falling into the serial waterfall trap but the most important attribute of whichever alternative you choose, it is vital to ensure that the accumulation of technical debt remains transparent. When it is transparent it can be monitored to ensure that the technical debt is not be allowed to grow too large.

---

[12] Some organizations choose to create a single Definition of Done but to identify which items are relevant at the story level and which are applicable at the release level. While the approach is somewhat different the effect is identical because the set of validations at the story and release are different

The most straightforward strategy for avoiding the serial waterfall trap is to not allow any story points to be banked until all of the Definition of Done items needed to release the story to production have been completed and validated. This is a difficult challenge though when there are separate Definitions of Done for stories and releases or sprints. One approach to managing this challenge and at the same time keep the technical debt backlog visible is to keep the story points for stories that have not yet been validated against all of the Definitions of Done in a pending state and to add this pending state to the team burn-down charts. This situation is illustrated in Figure 24.

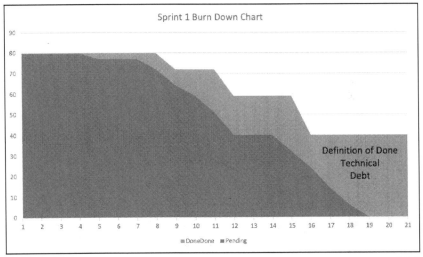

Figure 24- The accumulation of Technical Debt can be made transparent using a model that only shows stories as done when they have been validated against all of the relevant Definitions of Done

The figure shows an example of a Sprint where the team had committed to deliver 80 Story Points. The bottom data set illustrates that over time stories are being completed and validated against the story level Definition of Done which completes on day 19 of the sprint. The top data set shows the burndown for stories that have been validated against both the story and the release levels of Definition of Done. The area between the two lines illustrates the accumulation of technical debt which of course has to be carried over into the team's subsequent sprint. The impact of carrying stories to subsequent sprints in the pending state is shown in

Figure 25. It is obvious that the additional effort to validate that the stories in a pending state will impact the team's velocity in subsequent sprints. It is exactly this accumulation of technical debt that can force teams to dedicate entire sprints to completing specific tasks.

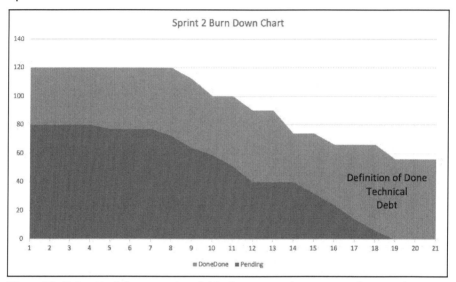

Figure 25 - It is critical that any technical debt due to stories being in a pending state be carried forward to subsequent sprints

As illustrated in Figures 24 and 25, keeping the accumulation of technical debt highly visible creates a compelling reminder of where a team really is with respect to actually being done-done with stories. It is also obvious from the example that it is not too difficult to imagine a situation where the technical debt can become overwhelming. We would not want to release software into a production environment that had not been validated against the non-functional dimensions of quality but that is what often happens and, because once the software is operational it becomes less likely that the team will pay any attention to the technical debt.

Another strategy for managing the story and release definitions of done is to create separate technical stories for completing the Release level Definitions of Done. In this model a story for validating the release component definition of done is added as the final story in each releasable component. This does provide visibility to the fact that there is still work remaining before a component can be released but it is not as clear about the magnitude of the work that may be remaining. Organizations that choose this strategy can sometimes fall into the trap of not adding a story at the end of each releasable component but of adding a single story to cover multiple release components. This is fine when release components of a single feature are being combined to make a larger component but becomes risky when the scope covers multiple features being worked on by a single team and dangerous when the single story covers features being worked on by multiple teams. This strategy is illustrated below.

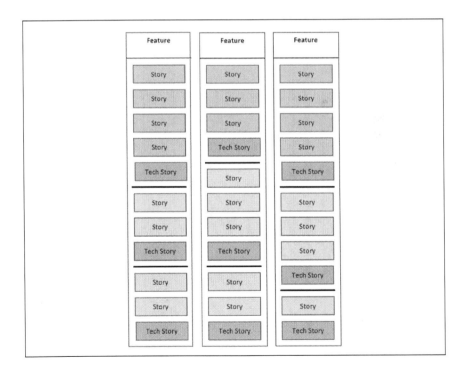

Figure 26 - Adding Technical Stories to the backlog at each release point is another strategy adding transparency to the Technical Debt backlog being accumulated by not completing the validation of both the story and release definitions of done

Restrict Technical Debt Growth

The second component of avoiding the Definition of Done serial waterfall trap is to limit the growth of your technical debt. There are many ways to restrict the growth of technical debt. One strategy is to limit how much technical debt may be accumulated by any team. The accumulation limit should be expressed as a percentage of the team's average sprint velocity. The closer an absolute restriction is to a team's average velocity the more likely it is that the team will fall into the serial waterfall trap.

A second strategy for restricting the technical debt growth is to require Product Owners to declare sets of stories that they deem releasable components and them not begin work on any new stories that are not part of the release set until they have first validated the completed set of stories against the release level definition of done. This approach is very consistent with the objective of always having the team working on the highest business value items. The grouping of stories into releasable sets is illustrated below.

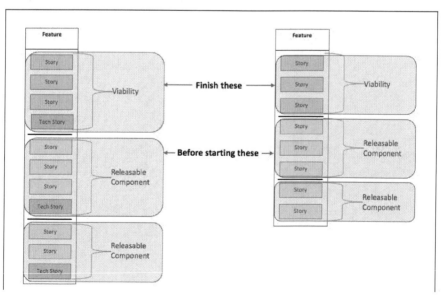

Figure 27 - By Grouping stories into releasable units and requiring teams to complete all levels of Definition of Done at the group level you can successfully restrict the growth of your Technical Debt. This principle is illustrated through the horizontal bars

Getting your Definition of Done right

A Definition of Done that focuses too much on activities rather than outcomes runs the risk of becoming more of a checklist than anything else. You don't want people to do things because they were told to do them, you want people doing things because they believe they are adding value. For example, a Definition of Done that specifies, as some do, that some percentage of code is formally reviewed, or some percent of Unit Test Coverage achieved, is addressing effort which is very different than addressing quality which should be the focus.

Empowering teams means giving them equal portions of responsibility and accountability and holding them responsible for achieving their outcomes. This is very different from holding them accountable for completing a series of activities that are not directly the outcome. A team might legitimately decide that all code that has a cyclomatic complexity exceeding a specific threshold must be code reviewed or must have a certain amount of automated unit test coverage but such a requirement should be decided on by the team and defined because the team believes that by doing those things will help them achieve the level of quality they are committed to. When the organization defines such criteria as part of the DoD, not only are they losing the focus on their outcomes, they are also disempowering the teams by telling them what to do rather than what they need to accomplish. It also puts a lot of the responsibility for reducing waste on the people telling the team what they are required to do. From the team's perspective it turns diagnostic metrics into outcome metrics which is not something we want to be doing.

Updating your Definition of Done

Any definition of done is a living document that needs to be updated to reflect changing operational circumstances and learnings. Often, the impetus for updating a Definition of Done will come out of a Root Cause Process triggered by a production incident but not every Root Cause action will impact your Definition of Done. It is a good practice to manage the growth of your Definition of Done. Every time a new item is added to your DoD it is a good idea to look at all of the items to ensure that each of the items and if there are items that can either never be detected in production or if detected would not result in a defect then those items do not belong in your DoD and should be removed.

Managing Defects

There is realistically no way to avoid defects in software projects. The process of how defects are managed needs to be defined and that begins with the creation of a Service Level Agreement (SLA). Any violation of the project's Definition of Done is considered a defect. Having a standard process for managing defects across the entire organization is necessary so that a debate about what to do with each defect can be avoided.

Defect SLA

The defect SLA defines how defects are prioritized and how teams are required to respond based on a defect's priority. Any violation of the organization's **Definition of Done** is a defect. This needs to be the case whether the defects are found in production or in testing. Defining and adhering to a defect SLA is necessary to ensuring customer satisfaction and is also required if we are going to correctly measure rework on our teams. The SLA needs to explicitly address the initial response to a defect being discovered and both the categorization of priorities and the team responses for each of the priorities. The SLA may also address communication around the status of a defect throughout the remediation process. All of the organization stakeholders need to agree on the SLA and engineering leadership needs to ensure compliance. Support organizations need to be included in the SLA development process because they are often the face to the customer. Successful implementation of our outcome metric depends on an SLA that compels the teams to address defects with a certain degree of urgency.

The defect SLA addresses defect priority rather than defect severity. To understand why we focus on priority rather than severity consider the following scenario. A severity 1 defect with significant revenue impact is reported on March 1. The Product Owner is immediately notified and determines that the defect is a Priority 1. Engineering is notified and immediately engages. They find the source of the defect and it is determined that the defect is specifically related to the leap year event and that it can only manifest itself on February 29. They notify the Product Owner who lowers the priority of the defect to P3 and leaving the severity at 1. Because the defect will not manifest itself again for nearly 4 years there is no immediate need for the engineering team to asynchronously interrupt their iteration to deal with fixing a defect that will not be seen for years. It is of course important that the defect be fixed before the next leap year but it is not important that it be fixed immediately.

It is important that all defects be expeditiously triaged and that Priority 1 and Priority 2 defects be moved into the team's backlogs so that they can be resolved as quickly as possible. The Priority 1 and 2 definitions are particularly important to get right because they define the defects that will interrupt work in the middle of an iteration. As difficult as it is, you want to be as unambiguous as possible in defining particularly the line between P1 and P2 but also the line between P2 and P3. It is common to see more than three levels of priority in a defect SLA but additional levels only add to the challenge of creating the unambiguous definitions without adding a lot of value. Any defect that does not rise above the P1 and P2 definitions will be considered when iteration commitments are being made and so adding additional priorities may not add any value.

Triaging of defects is the responsibility of Product Owners and it is something they should be doing every day. The triage process looks at the severity and impact of a defect and assigns a priority. It is the priority, not the severity assigned to a defect that dictates how quickly the defect makes it into a team's backlog. While team responses to defects is governed by the priority assigned to the defect the product owner's response has to be governed by the severity of the defect. Product owners need to immediately triage any severity 1 or 2 defect that is reported.

Priority	Description	Team Response
1	One or more critical system functions are not available Immediate security vulnerability or incident detected Immediate impact on ability to generate or collect revenue	Team interrupts what it is going and immediately assigns whatever resources needed to resolve the issue and works it until it is resolved. Defect resolution takes precedent over all other team activities.
2	One or more non-critical system function not available Critical system function not meeting SLA or causing high numbers of customer contacts	Team assigns whatever resources needed to resolve the issue and works it until it is resolved as the next work item started. Defect takes precedence over any new story.
3	Non-critical system function causing customer contacts No revenue impact	Team considers business value of fixing defect against other work items in its backlog during sprint planning

Figure 28 – Sample SLA. Having a non-ambiguous defect Service Level Agreement plays a big role in ensuring that defects are given the attention they need to receive[13]

Contained Defects?

Contained defects are good things! Any defect detected and resolved by engineers prior to declaring the code to be complete is a contained defect. When there are testers on teams any defect discovered by the testers should not be considered a contained defect. Defects found by testers on teams were leaked by engineers and as such contribute to waste. While defects

[13] Since any defect other than P1 and P2 gets put into a queue and are evaluated in terms of business value when teams are committing stories to iterations it is really not necessary to define more than 3 levels

found by testers on teams may not need to be treated using the same SLA used for production defects or defects found by external testing teams they still fall into the class of defects that were discovered after an engineer declared his or her code to be complete.

Some teams may choose to count the number of defects they are able to contain and the methods by which they were contained although that data is generally not reliable. Some tools used by the teams may automatically gather some of the contained defect data and in those cases the data is more reliable. Teams may also choose to categorize the types of defects they are containing as such data can be useful in identifying training opportunities. The number and types of defects being contained as well as the containment activity that identified them are data points that the team may use to help them improve. They are also items that may provide insight during CompStat reviews.

Intentionally Leaked Defects

Whether you have testers on teams or independent testing teams there are almost always going to be situations where defects that were discovered during testing are not significant enough to stop the release of the software. Defects found during testing need to be triaged as if they were found on the live site. In thise cases where the Product Owner prioritizes a defect as either a Priority 1 or 2 the team needs to respond to the defect in accordance with the SLA. In most cases, lower priority defects can be put into the defect queue to be reviewed in subsequent iteration commitment sessions.

Learning from Defects

The only real value we have from defects is the opportunity to learn. That said, it does not make sense to try to investigate the root cause of a leaked defect. Doing so is always going to result in a finding of either inadequate processes, human error, or someone not following a process. While there may be some cases, medically implanted devices come to mind, where there is an extremely high cost associated with any failure, where it is necessary to carry out a root cause investigation, trying to root cause a defect is almost always a waste of time. There is, however, value in looking at what might have been done to prevent the defect from leaking. High performing teams will want to ask themselves this question for all priority 1 and 2 defects as they will have had a direct impact on the team's ability to meet the commitment they made in the previous iteration.

While executing a root cause process on defects is unlikely to lead to any process changes that does not mean teams can not learn from their leaked defects. As part of the defect resolution it is perfectly appropriate and helpful for the team to use their iteration retrospectives to review the defects that asynchronously interrupted their iteration to ask themselves what they might have done to avoid leaking the defect. Where there are independent testing teams they need to also learn what they might have done differently to have detected the defect prior to it having been released.

Resolved Defects

Resolved defects need to be thoroughly validated before the remediated software is deployed onto the live site. It looks very bad when a defect is believed to have been resolved and in fact it was not. It is also very bad when a defect reappears after it had been resolved. The probability of preventing either of these scenarios from occurring can be improved by taking actions such as ensuring that defects are fully understood and that the steps to reproduce any high priority defect are well defined. It is also a good practice for all high priority defects to require that an automated test be created that would detect the defect should it ever be reintroduced.

Continuous Integration and Deployment

The time it takes for code to move from an engineer's workstation into testing environments and ultimately onto a live site is a common source of waste and often of complexity. While engineers are not likely to sit and do nothing while they are waiting for software to be deployed to test and production environments the more complex a system you have the higher the probability that something could go wrong. When something does go wrong engineers are often called on to work on fixing deployment issues which is an asynchronous interruption and an instance of waste.

Certainly our focus is on engineering productivity but we can not ignore the need for support organizations such as DevOps which is primarily responsible for developing and operating the engineering pipeline all teams need if they are going to successfully implement Continuous Integration (CI) and Continuous Deployment (CD) infrastructures.

Developing an engineering pipeline is no easy feat. It is a complex engineering challenge and often requires significant investments in time and money. The return on the investment is significant both in terms of reducing waste and risk. Virtualization of servers and databases has made developing and maintaining engineering pipelines significantly easier than it had been. The technologies make environments on demand a realistic concept. Virtualization also brings with it the opportunity to do things such as always building on clean machines and easily turning off environments when they are not being used simple tasks to accomplish.

It is beyond the scope of this book to go into how an engineering pipeline can be designed and implemented. Questions such as how many environments are needed in the pipeline and whether each team needs its own environment are ones that have to be dealt with based on the situation and complexity of the system.

Conclusion

Software projects are going to continue to be difficult to predict. But if we always have our teams focusing on the highest business value items and focus on eliminating waste we can be confident that we will consistently improve both the quantity and the quality of our software products.

Clearly there is neither a silver bullet nor a secret sauce that will provide everybody the answers they would like to have when it comes to software development. The desire to have those answers will undoubtably persist and perhaps some day the answer will emerge. But that reality should not keep us from what we can achieve which is to improve our execution and be able to demonstrate that we are indeed improving.

So if I return to the basic three questions that we need to answer we will confidently be able to answer:

Q1. Are we better now than we were?
A. Yes.
Q2. Are we going to be better than we are now?
A. Yes.
Q3. How do we know?
A. Because we are measuring waste which is something objective and can see that our teams are wasting less which means they are spending more time producing software and adding business value

Made in the USA
San Bernardino, CA
05 December 2018